D0862059

STAN PERSKY

Buddy's

MEDITATIONS ON DESIRE

NEW STAR BOOKS ‖ VANCOUVER

Copyright © 1989, 1991 by Stan Persky

All rights reserved. No part of this work may be reproduced or used in any form or by any means – graphic, electronic, or mechanical – without the prior written permission of the publisher. Any request for photocopying or other reprographic copying must be sent in writing to the Canadian Reprography Collective, 379 Adelaide St. W., Suite M1, Toronto, Ont. M5V 1S5.

The photo on page 73 is used with the permission of Pink Triangle Press and Rick Bebout.

First trade paperback printing April 1991
1 2 3 4 5   95 94 93 92 91
Printed and bound in Canada
Printed on acid-free paper

The publisher is grateful for assistance provided by the Canada Council and the Cultural Services Branch, Province of British Columbia

New Star Books Ltd.
2504 York Avenue
Vancouver, British Columbia
Canada V6K 1E3

Canadian Cataloguing in Publication Data
Persky, Stan, 1941-
Buddy's
ISBN 0-921586-19-1
1. Homosexuality, Male. 2. Gay men. I. Title.
HQ76.P48 1991   306.7'662   C91-091285-8

Contents

III
Darkness

homage à Roland Barthes;
for George Stanley

Buddy's

BUDDY'S was a two-storey gay bar tucked into a side street at the edge of Vancouver's West End, just off one of the main thoroughfares leading into downtown. The location had housed a series of unsuccessful clubs and bars over the years, but its most recent incarnation appeared to have caught on, at least for the time being. The current owners had established an institutional identity somewhere between the compulsiveness of the Gandydancer and the exotic sleaze of downtown pubs like the Ambassador or the Dufferin. Buddy's appealed largely to "upwardly mobile" middle class gays, as the aspiring were momentarily known.

The ground floor contained a spacious conversation bar decorated in an all-purpose tropical style and bathed in peach light. Upstairs was a dimly lit narrow room which combined elements of Dante's worst premonitions with aspects of an overgrown Boys' Club – a feat that seems to be a specialty of gay commercial culture. The dance floor was at the front, the pool table in the back.

I'd been to Buddy's a few times, and often on my way home I drove by with the half-formed intention of stopping in for a drink. Usually, though, the plan was abandoned after making a feeble pass in search of a non-existent parking space. But this was Saturday night, about ten o'clock, the moon was almost full, and anyway, it was the beginning of autumn. That meant there were months of cold, rainy days ahead, a succession of permanent mid-afternoons with low cloud ceilings that would blot out the North Shore mountains for weeks at a time. And, of course, there was an available parking space.

I WAS UPSTAIRS, in back by the pool table, nursing a scotch and soda. I idly watched the pool players. The sound system throbbed monotonously, altering its beat slightly every few minutes, attempting to maintain, above all, a seamless web that might keep us fixed in this temporary eternal reality. The hit tune that season, I seem to recall, was something called "Masterpiece." *Life is a movie/You gotta try it*, it wailed to the dancers at the far end of the room.

Some time before, while having a drink here, I'd spotted a blond kid at the pool table and now I hoped, though without much urgency, that he would reappear. The week already looked pretty full and I was content to let Buddy's wash over me. The pool players pursued their singular objects. One or two of them were faintly familiar from other bars, other nights. The disco gradually filled. Behind the bar, an electronic sign (I think it's called a "reader board") announced future "happy hours," and blinkingly informed us that "Sylvain is your barman, Brian is your waiter ..." A busboy, who didn't make the reader board, was wearing a tank top, athletic shorts, and calf-length white socks: at a distance it was like seeing a mirage of a fifteen-year-old basketball player.

I'd almost decided to leave when I found myself engulfed in a one-sided breathless conversation. "Oh no, I couldn't tell you, it wouldn't be fair," he was saying, "and oh, it would take too long." He made it seem as though he would have to provide a detailed explanation of every major event in his life in order to properly account for his present distress. "Oh, I'm Jay, what's your name?"

"Couldn't tell me what?" I asked. I saw that I would always be a couple of sentences behind in any conversation with Jay, who had already gone on to introduce me to three or four people he was with. I was shaking hands with a couple of shadowy strangers whose names I'd missed, while Jay was explaining that Gary, the nearest young man, was going with – the name went by me – one of the pool players, and indeed, after missing a shot, the other young man came over to us and he and Gary were soon wrapped around each other. The lovers, handsome and athletic, seemed drawn from a college football team's backfield. All of Jay's friends had a kind of indistinguishable but appealing neatness about them. They had blow-dried bird-feather haircuts and were already wearing windbreakers for fall, like advertisements for Eaton's or the Bay. All, that is, except Jay.

Jay was a brown-skinned lean young man in his early twenties who claimed to be an Indian from the Cariboo. He had an unruly mop of black hair that hadn't been tamed in a unisex salon, vast liquid brown eyes, and unlike his more fashionable age-mates, was wearing a checkered flannel mackinaw, jeans and a loose fitting white T-shirt with large punk-style rips in it through which patches of his chamois brown torso were visible.

"So, what exactly is wrong?" I persisted, cutting into his incessant and charming stream of chatter. Well, it seemed Jay had borrowed 50 dollars from someone and had only paid back about half of it. He had been told to be in Buddy's at eleven with the rest, but of course didn't have it. The upshot was, "And, if I don't have it, John is going to beat me up." Jay said all this in tones of theatrical but genuine dismay, mixed with what I thought was a tinge of being thrilled by the prospect.

Several questions crowded my mind. "He's going to beat you up for twenty dollars?" It seemed like an incredibly small amount in these inflationary times. "Who is he? And if you don't have it, then what are you doing here?"

"Oh yes, look what he already did to me," Jay said, twisting his head to display a bruised lip as he launched into an account of his complex, lengthy association with John, who was, despite all, "really nice," and who would, if Jay tried to escape, "find me anyway." John was made to sound like the head of the local branch of an inexorable mafia capable of tracking Jay to the ends of the earth. "So I've got to get twenty dollars by eleven . . . Oh, I mean, you wouldn't, would you?" Jay gasped in feigned or real disbelief.

"Okay," I said.

"You will?" Jay seemed authentically surprised. "But why? You don't even know me. Oh, what time is it?"

It was a few minutes before eleven. As for why, I had no idea. Certainly, this snap decision wasn't characteristic of my normally deliberative wariness. Nor was it desire. Desire was the blond kid who hadn't shown up. Maybe it was respect for sublunar events, one of my few superstitions. In any case, it was such an unusual come-on, if it was a come-on, that I was amused and engrossed. It was only after the fact that I realized I had agreed to have sex with Jay.

"What do you do?" Jay asked before I'd finished answering the last barrage of queries.

"I write books, and teach – "

"Do you publish?" Jay wanted to know.

"Yes, sure." In fact, I was more or less "between books" at the moment – a polite phrase that organized wads of psychic chaos. "And I teach at – "

"What kind of books do you write? Because I'm writing a book, too. It's about being a male prostitute," Jay burbled.

"Well," I said, raising my glass of melted icecubes and passing him a twenty, "from one writer to another."

Sure enough, in about five minutes, John arrived. I don't know what kind of a thumb-breaker I was expecting. John was a conventionally handsome young man, the same age as the rest of Jay's friends, the same fashionably cropped haircut, and he wore a jacket which said that his team had won last year's softball tournament. He exchanged greetings with Jay's friends, which made me naively wonder why they hadn't bothered to rescue him. In fact, John appeared to be a member of their circle. I was introduced and shook hands with him. John semi-apologized to Jay for having slugged him earlier, but when the money was handed over, he said with appropriate menace, "It's a good thing you've got it, 'cause there's three guys waiting downstairs." Since Jay was hardly a match for John, these three

6

off-stage enforcers represented either the spirit of vengeance or a sign of organizational obsessiveness. The whole transaction took place quickly and was no more dramatic than a dope delivery. Nonetheless, the entire performance, however stilted, had to be rated a cut above your ordinary non-eventful evening in a gay bar.

"Whew!" Jay sighed after John had melted away.

"Feel better?"

"Oh, do I ever. Here, feel my heart," Jay said, pulling up his T-shirt for an instant and pressing my hand to his chest. Somehow, touching his flesh startled me, broke through what was, up to then, the sort of scene you might half-attentively watch on television. "I've got to have a drink and a couple of dances before we go." On the dance floor, Jay's slinky movement brought to mind a Shiva statue I'd once seen with my friend George in a Seattle museum. The multi-coloured spots in the ceiling flickered and pulsated, cutting the dancers into a cubist tableau. Meanwhile, the world went on. The sound system throbbed a bit more frenetically, the pool players moved in slow motion through their aqueous universe, the bar became crowded.

WE CUT into the southbound traffic flow, travelling over the hump of Burrard bridge, which connects the downtown peninsula to the shores of Kitsilano. The moon was behind the Molson Brewery clock tower at the south end of the bridge. It was midnight.

I lived a block above Kits beach, in a large, gloomy, old house shared by a half-dozen people. Jay and I stood on the front steps looking out across the dark water to the glitter of West Vancouver. He was impressed by the view.

The sex was bound to be anti-climactic. We stripped and got into bed. "I can't kiss because of this," Jay said, indicating his puffy lip. "What do you like to do?" he asked. I vacillated. "I mean, really," Jay insisted.

This was just before we knew about the plague, which was then but an ominous rumour. "Well, these days I like getting fucked."

"Oh," Jay said, dismayed, "so do I."

I laughed at this impasse. "Well, we'll manage."

I ran my hand along his smooth, tan body, and went down on him. Jay's cock promptly hardened into a medium-sized horn that curved toward his belly. I caressed his inner thigh and ran my fingers into the crack of his ass. "Do you want a finger up there?" I asked, coming up for air.

"But not a handful," Jay said, as I reached for the K-Y lubricant. "At least not to start with," he coyly amended. I slowly slid my finger into him and went back to what I'd been doing. Jay couldn't blow me because of his battered mouth, so he turned over on his belly. His bum was small and cushiony, rising and falling in response to my rhythm.

WE TIP-TOED out of the sleeping house, pausing again on the front steps. "If you remember to ask me, I'll tell you a secret when we're in the car," Jay said.

I turned on the heater to protect him from the middle-of-the-night chill as we pulled away from the house. Jay was still puzzled about what had happened earlier in the evening. "But why did you give me the money? You didn't have to."

"I don't know. It was an intuition."

We were driving along the park that bordered Kits beach. "What's the secret?" I asked. I couldn't remember when I'd last heard someone use the word "secret."

"Oh," Jay said, as if he had forgotten. "I was thinking I wouldn't mind waking up and seeing that view from your house in the morning."

I was momentarily flustered. "Well, look, we – I mean, I'll turn around –"

"No, no, it's too late now. It's okay," Jay assured me.

Again, he had succeeded in amusing and touching me. I dropped Jay off near Buddy's, made a U-turn on the traffic-free boulevard, and headed home. The moon had moved on, no doubt giving other people unexpected intuitions.

* * *

I WAS GOING to write a series of tales, matter-of-factly relating erotic encounters which originated in Buddy's. They were to be composed in a mock-pornographic style, which is to say, whereas pornographic prose merely aims at arousal, these accounts, while adhering to the conventions of the genre, would nonetheless present *persons* – that is, they would seek to intrigue by recognizing the complexity of experience, the very thing that porn must resolutely avoid, lest it suffer the decomposition of its stereotypes, and thus its reason for being.

The story about Jay was to be the first of them. I showed a first draft to George, but he didn't like it. I decided it was a failure. So I put it away in a drawer. Now, slightly revised, a little less arch, it returns, or it is permitted to reappear, at least as documentary.

Let it serve, then, as the beginning of these meditations on desire, discourse, darkness. They invoke the locales and language of the homoerotic. But, of course, they're not intended solely for those who share that particular sexual "preference" – which is, in fact, not a preference, but a passion. Rather, they're motivated by the "desire and pursuit of the whole," to recall the half-comic definition of love that Aristophanes offers in Plato's *Symposium*. Since they arrive in a time of plague, they are shadowed by elegy. As in our conversations these days, even when the pestilence goes unspoken, we let it underlie everything.

THE DESIRE, then, to rescue all failed works. Yet it is, admittedly, a utopian fantasy: the idea that no part of the work is ultimately rejected.

Similarly, my refusal to abandon any former lover. When someone I loved and/or slept with turns up years later for lunch, now married, parental, embarked upon a surprising vocation, my response is invariably one of pleasure. However fragile, I retrieve the utopian image: love is endless.

Desire, fortunately, isn't. I look into the face of the loved one, puzzled, unable to find a ghost of what turned me on. Or, the slim basketball player – was his name Jim? – appears on the doorstep, years afterward, as a portly, middle aged electronics salesman, wanting to strike up an old relationship. And all I can remember is what a fuss he made in bed at the zenith of his beauty, having to insist that he wasn't gay even as I was entangled in his limbs, or announcing after some intimate act – had he just blown me? – that "I don't usually do that."

Yet, even as I mock the ghost, I also honour the image, recalling as well the night in a crowded bar when he sat on a high stool, his long dangling legs spread apart, and I backed into him, pressing my butt against his groin, signalling my submission to him, and to all who cared to see. But since the flame that took me was predicated upon desire rather than love, when I look into the hearthplace of the heart, I find no glowing embers, only cold ashes. At least *that* dies, I sigh, strangely contented.

I
Desire

Beauty

JEAN-PAUL SARTRE said, "My ugliness is certainly something I have to chalk up to fate, or what I might call the brutality of fate. Because: why was I born ugly? It's when you're dealing with such things that you see both contingency and brutality."

Coincidentally, on the facing page of the text where he says that (*Sartre By Himself*), there's a photo taken in 1945 in which he is standing at the end of a bridge of the kind that span the Seine in Paris. The background is almost entirely obscured in fog or mist. In the foreground, largely cropped out of the picture except for a Nordic face and a bit of the shoulder seen mostly from behind, is another man facing Sartre.

The philosopher is sucking on a pipe, cradling the warm bowl between his thumb, middle and index fingers, perhaps drawing comfort from its heat on what appears to be a chill, damp afternoon or late morning. Sartre's lips are lush and flat; his hair, in which streaks of a lighter colour appear, is neatly combed; a scarf is tied in a cravat covering his throat; he is wearing a vaguely military-style jacket or topcoat with a fur collar (a fashion which again became popular in the 1980s). His brow is furrowed, his mouth thoughtfully drawn, and behind his glasses, his right eye looks away, as though he is considering a question asked by the man in the foreground.

It is only on second glance that one notices that Sartre's left eye *isn't* looking away. Maybe it is that splayed sight that Sartre thinks of as his ugliness. For otherwise he is, as he says in the same text that people "ought to be," ordinary looking.

"Someone who thinks of himself or herself as handsome or beautiful," Sartre continues, "has to assume a stance, an attitude of body alienation, of the *sacralization* of the body, and what is more, he or she then has a need to be noticed by others, since beauty is something others bestow on you."

13

YET WHAT struck me about the young men or boys I was attracted to in my youth was that they apparently didn't know they were beautiful. This seemed to me incredible. But they were invariably unaware of their beauty. I once asked a former beloved, "Did you know that you were beautiful?" "Not until you told me," he demurely replied. Today, advertising has made them aware of their market value.

Of course, much of this is determined by a social grammar. Our culture forces girls and young women from their earliest days to consider their "looks." For males, however, when I was growing up, there wasn't even an available vocabulary by which to raise the matter. The two inadequate words given to us were "good-looking" and "handsome." The latter merely means dextrous, as in "handyman." It's not that some men aren't "handsome"; rather, I object to the way "handsome" is used to suppress other words that might be taken to signal desire. Girls were permitted to say a boy was "cute," as they did about A. in his powder blue V-neck sweater at the junior prom, but boys couldn't say that about other boys. Even today, when B., who is himself beautiful, notices another pretty youth and says, "He's cute," the very word stirs me. Homoerotic desire is founded not only on forbidden recognitions, but also on a repressed lexicon.

This contingency of "fate" – the arbitrariness by which the other is born beautiful – seemed to me grossly unfair. I saw it not as accident, but as a cause for moral outrage. The beautiful one "has it easy"; "he can have anything he wants without even trying." Unless, it turns out, what he wants can't be gotten by beauty. In the end, then, this cosmic injustice evens out. Beauty "fades." More important, though, as can be seen in Buddy's, where many of the young men (often hustlers) have had their beauty validated as a commodity, they want to be liked *for themselves*. "He wants me for more than just sex," one alluring beauty accusingly said to me in the upstairs bar one night.

It seems absurd: there is so little difference between one human nose and another; the line of *his* torso compared to that other's; the sight of the thighs of the boy in shorts – the one who climbed up a tree . . .

This happens in the midst of an anti-nuke demo in Vancouver; I'm part of a crowd of 50,000 people. Yet, I notice I'm reluctant to sketch in the larger context in which the erotic glimpse occurs. It's as if in order to attend to the amorous quest, I have to bracket off these citizenly duties. I seem to want a sort of holiday: from politics, business, vocation, even from the endemic hostility society accords this passion. But, of course, there is no holiday. Entranced by a half-clad youth who has climbed into the branches of a tree, it is the case that we are part of a peace demonstration; we belong to history even in the utter privacy of desire. So, those honey-tan thighs – and I am back to the contradiction: though it is not an absolute, I would rather see him than a sunset. Yet we make such a fuss over these distinctions.

I'm perplexed: beauty is apparently not an absolute; it too is subject to fashion. Or: people disagree about whether so-and-so is beautiful. "I don't know what you see in him." And reduced to a disappointing relativity: it is said to be in the eye of the beholder. I can't imagine a less reliable place for it.

The absurdity becomes more apparent when I direct my attention to species other than human which attract me: e.g., antelopes; so far, all antelopes are beautiful to me.

I Could Write A Book

B'S FRIEND, Ian, formerly his lover, phones to enquire about B. Although Ian and I are barely acquainted, we fall into a lengthy discussion. Actually, it's a monologue or recital by Ian. B. had lived with this middle aged man, on and off, for about two years. At one point in our conversation, the task of explaining this relationship presents itself to Ian as so overwhelming that he blurts out, "Oh, I could write a book about all that's happened." Since I write books, when someone says that sentence to me, I imagine that he *has* written a book and that I am reading it.

Montaigne

A SURPRISING number of my friends and acquaintances who hustle propose that their life stories could be "written up" or would "make a good book." I'm never bored by the prospect of these erotic histories. Immediately, I concede to their would-be authors the sincerity of a Montaigne, who was "prepared to give a full-length, and quite naked, portrait" of himself. I imagine a genre of true *autopornographies*.

Decor

OUTSIDE, there is a discreet, purple neon sign with the word "Buddy's" written in jaunty script. Neon, a technology common to a previous generation, is once more in vogue; it's "very eighties." As it glows in the mild summer night, this design conveys more than information, it connotes a series of meanings.

It suggests, to me at least, allure, clandestinity, pick-ups of the sexual sort, sin even . . . but also casualness, "let's have a drink after work," "*class*," says my friend George, rendezvous, as in, "I'm off to my assignation," modishness – in short, a certain style. The possible messages which the "Buddy's" sign sends are intentionally multiple, but not unrestricted. It seeks to lure a variable clientele, yet it offers no invitation, for example, to the leather-sheathed gay biker – although occasionally one is seen wandering through here, not unwelcome, but as exotic as a diplomat from Mordor.

The downstairs bar, which, as a friend remarked, has the air of a "drawing room," is marked by levels, nooks-and-crannies, sites, zones. Two steps down from the dark foyer into a spacious, well-lighted room, about 30 metres in length . . . but immediately on the left, two steps up, a platform with a railing, containing two rows of tightly packed tiny tables. The waiter, usually Brinko, has to wriggle through, tray held aloft, to deliver the drinks. It's a kind of balcony from which one can view the passing parade just below, as if it were History, or ignoring the hurly-burly, lean forward engrossed in a tête-à-tête. Across the main concourse – actually just an aisle – the bar itself, a massive roccoco affair; the sideboard behind it is an arrangement of polished wooden columns topped with carved acanthus leaves; arches, mirrors, displays.

Beyond that, an area of larger tables and chairs, a cozy corner with a fireplace in which a blaze is kept alight during the chill coastal rainy season, and next to the sloping corridor leading to the bathrooms, another opening with a sort of dutch-door affair that alternates between being a kitchen before 10 p.m. and something called a "shooter" bar which attracts a cluster of drinkers later in the evening. As well, here and there, like islands, box-like electronic devices whose floating liquid crystal figures give the appearance of a dark aquarium, which invariably draw, intentionally so, a pretty youth gazing into its pool. I'd often find M. or B. there, lost in contemplation of imaginary asteroids. The walls are decorated with closely spaced, small, framed pictures. The scenes portrayed are hardly memorable; rather, their function is to suggest the sedate nineteenth century calm of a gentleman's club. The entire room is bathed in a convivial pastel-coloured light.

The upstairs bar has a dance floor at one end and a pool table at the other. It lies under the traditional aegis of darkness and half-light common to gay discos, provided by ceiling spots, the pool table light, and an elaborate, swirling, pulsating contraption that illuminates the dancers.

You get to the "upper deck," as I once heard it jovially referred to, either by the steep, narrow, enclosed staircase off the foyer which emerges onto the edge of the dance floor (a further flight of stairs behind a door leads to a penthouse where management has its offices), or, at the end of the downstairs bar, a broad stairway with tubular metal railings that brings one to the pool players – an arrangement that permits customers to freely circulate through the two-storey building.

The place I prefer is a high table along the windows of the east wall. From there, one is afforded a clear view of the slow drama at the pool table and, at the same time, it's possible to monitor the arrival of those coming up the back staircase. The window, covered by a thin-slatted modern Venetian blind, looks into a windbreak of tall silver poplars. During the rainy season, the small wet leaves glisten under the coloured spotlights attached to the outside of the building.

THUS, night after night, consciously or otherwise, I studied the decor of Buddy's, taking the definition of that word, rooted in the Latin *decoris* ("beauty"), most literally: "all that makes up the appearance of a room or the stage." The bar is subject to a constant fussiness and spurts of redecoration. One week a piano on a tiny stage materialized in the downstairs lounge, as if someone had had a sudden haphazard recollection of piano bars. It soon vanished. Another time, after a two-week absence on summer holidays, I entered Buddy's to find the downstairs filled with beach umbrellas and other Riviera adornments; the patrons had been encouraged to wear shorts or beach wear, and loveable lemmings that we are, many had complied. The effect was dizzying. However, the weather soon changed, and a more placid rhythm replaced the short-lived frenzy.

Under the rule of this decor, a certain decorum is elicited. No brawls at Buddy's; even obstreperous drunks are discouraged; dress codes are unenforced but generally observed. Sexy costumes – shorts and tank tops – are welcome, as is New Wave fashion, middle class anonymous summerwear (pinstripe shirts and cords), and jogging sweats. Occasionally the bar appears to be populated by a roomful of toddlers in p.j.'s ready for bedtime.

At bottom, however, it is a careful class-based social mix that ensures the bar's success. Among the young, for example, the shadings between youthful working class gays, the hustlers who congregate around the pool table (a lumpenproletariat), and various bar personnel are contrived to be more or less indistinguishable, producing a tantalizing ambience of the unattainable and the available. Moreover, their own infrarelationships add texture to the situation: a former hustler begins working as a busboy; another busboy about to become a student has as a lover a pool player who works as a carpenter's helper. Similarly, the men in their thirties and forties, mostly middle class, who are simply socializing with their set – which includes a certain amount of ogling at and gossiping about the beauties – and those engaged in more practical pursuits ("chickenhawks") both present a homogenous well-behaved face; in short, a general and recognizable civility is achieved.

Between the decor and decorum are two mediating orders of officialdom: the discreet presence of management and the public one of the waiters, especially Brian and Brinko. Hieratic figures, guardians, Egyptian temple attendants, I marvel at the equanimity of their temperaments, their skills, the complementarity of their distinctive styles. Brinko, as his name suggests, is more a figure of fun; he camps, but there is a discernible toughness under that exterior. A street tough I used to trick with told me once, with admiration, how Brinko took up shooting pool, quickly moving from novice to formidable competitor. When he bustles about, tray in hand, briskly asking, "Everything okay?", a parody of the perfect hostess, and I joke, "Well . . . not *every*thing," he lifts an eyebrow and giggles, as if to assure me, I know *exactly* what you mean. Brian, the youthful blond who works upstairs, projects an endearing intimacy, softly touching your knee or inner thigh with his hand as he collects your order, draping an arm over your shoulder as he stops to chat during a lull. In contrast to the impersonal service found in straight pubs, here everyone colludes in the amorous project.

The mode of management is inevitably feudal. Even though I don't know the bar owners, I'm almost certain that is true, having worked as a bartender long ago. It's a world of retainers, favourites (the new doorman), jealousies/loyalties, whims, acts of arbitrary imperiousness. Occasionally, one of these rulers will make a brief public service appearance, when, for example, Buddy's is the location for the gay softball awards presentation. But the feudal power of the administration always threatens to become irrational, to reveal itself in the aspect of the "mad king."

I WAS WATCHING P. shooting pool, his opponent a frenetic but skilful middle aged patron rumoured to be a millionaire computer engineer, when a slightly drunken man in a Hawaiian shirt sidled up to me. It was a typical night at Buddy's; around the pool table was scattered a representative collection of strikingly attractive young men.

"Everybody's struttin' their stuff," the man in the Hawaiian shirt grumbled.

"What about him?" I asked, hoping to deflect the protester by pointing to a man across the room who was also, coincidentally, wearing an ill-fitting Hawaiian shirt.

"No, not him," conceded the critic. But he was not to be dissuaded, citing a litany of sins: the youths' blow-dried hair, their "tight-ass designer jeans," tanned limbs, etc. Of course, this was rather like going to a flower show and resenting the roses for their beauty. The clincher, apparently, was that for all the trouble they'd taken with their primping, they were still uncertain of their identities, had but disguised their condition, were no better than the rest of us, and so on. Although this was probably true, in fact, as I glanced around, I noticed little out of the ordinary, nor did it appear that anyone had taken special pains, except perhaps for one lad, who had formerly worn sweatshirts with a marsupial pouch and had recently acquired a rather pleasing preppie look. But my complainant was not to be mollified.

He was determined to have the last word, and did: "This place oozes sex."

Indeed. The whole point of the setting is to engender an erotic *élan*: it is, then, an official decor of desire. But let's not be overly euphoric. Another night: the bar fills with statuesque types in cut-offs, and even an unusually noisy queen. Insufferable boredom. It's like a fitness shop. And yet . . . here something slightly unexpected occurs to engage my faculties . . . and I'm aroused from my torpor. A beautiful blond youth materializes. He seems aloof, worshippable only at a distance. Imperceptibly, dancing begins around him. Soon, he's dancing too. Then, without warning, he pulls off his shirt, revealing a gleaming torso. Nonetheless, in the midst of my delight – the bar arrives at a moment of perfection – a paradox: this effusion of orchestrated decor is a constraint, a confining obsession, the perverse of the free-forms of Eros.

There's a Buddy's in every large North American city that seeks a return on capital from investment in this illusion. Nor is it confined to the homoerotic. Heterosexual versions of this apparition abound as well. These easily replicable milieus of desire are practically a form of franchise capitalism. Buddy's is a gay bar, but it's also a text, an irony, a homophone. It offers the mirage of friendship under impossible conditions. Yet, on some nights, improbably enough, it delivers. When it does, Buddy's is buddies.

Faggot

ONE OF THE MOST beautiful of the homoerotic figures: a wraith-like creature breezing through the almost empty upstairs bar at Buddy's (early evening), one shoulder raised, head thrown back, arms half-wrapped around the torso like folded birdwings. In some, this sight inspires revulsion, expletives, the urge to violence. For me, his "walk" bears the *woundedness* of centuries of disdain, history as gesture, "bloodied but unbowed."

Sememe

PETER, an attractive hustler shooting pool at Buddy's, stretches his body over the worn felt-covered table to make a shot. As he does so, his jeans pull tightly around his ass while his black T-shirt draws upward in the reaching movement of his arms. Unexpectedly, an inch or two of tanned flesh flashes before our eyes in the space between the two items of apparel. A moment of stasis or still-life: Peter is sprawled/taut; vulnerable/poised; then there's a click of pool balls. He straightens up, his T-shirt readjusts itself, skin disappears, he steps back into the shadows. If the smallest unit of meaning in the science of signs can be called a sememe, then the glimpse is the smallest unit of meaning in the composition of desire.

Or: "Is not the most erotic portion of a body *where the garment gapes?*" asks Roland Barthes. " . . . skin flashing between two articles of clothing . . . it is this flash which seduces, or rather: the staging of an appearance-as-disappearance." The conjunction of reading that fragment (the other day) and of seeing Peter appears to me as a demonstrated proof of Barthes' assertion, almost a replication of scientific findings.

Plato's *Charmides*: " . . . at that moment, my good friend, I caught a sight of the inwards of his garment, and took the flame. Then I could no longer contain myself."

Shimmel

"HAVE YOU noticed those T-shirts boys are wearing this summer – the ones that only come down part-way?" I asked George. He hadn't. We were down from Vancouver for the day to visit his brother in Seattle.

The first time I'd seen one was in Buddy's a couple of weeks earlier. A young man at the pool table was in a sleeveless gray T-shirt that came to just below the rib cage, providing a constant view of bared skin between the unexpected end of his top and the faded jeans that sinuously clung to his hips.

Momentarily obsessed by the nomenclature of this half-topless item in the fashion system, I went into a sporting goods shop, leaving George and his brother on the sidewalk, to ask what these shirts were called. "Schimmels," said the saleswoman without hesitation. She spelled it for me. "But what are they for?" I asked disingenuously, wanting a semi-official ideological explanation. "It's just a summer fad," she answered evasively. Well, what could you expect?: "It's to make boys look sexier"? In a consumer society that devours "entertainment" rather than seeking "happiness," there must be euphemisms for all aspects of desire, even its vestments.

"Schimmels," I announce, rejoining George and his brother on the street. The mystery only deepened. In the next block, I dragged them into a bookstore. I love these inconsequential manias. "Schimmel," according to the not-very-helpful German dictionary, had something to do with "mold, mildew, a sour smell." We attempt to piece it out. Sweat! That's the sour smell. It must be a colloquial word meaning something like "sweatshirt." Browsing through a newspaper one afternoon, I even found an ad for "shimmels" – the "c" unaccountably absent.

Used by football players during summer practice scrimmages

(I had seen them on TV sports clips), they were meant to prevent chafing by the shoulder pads and to provide a bit of cool relief in the pre-season heat. But worn in the bar or on the streets, the shimmel's function is purely mannerist, permanently displaying the flesh that in ordinary movement is only momentarily and seductively revealed.

I point out several boys on the street wearing them. "There," I say excitedly, like an explorer in the Great Plains of Semiotica locating a long-sought species of fauna. George at last sees. "Bare midriff T-shirts," George nods. "Designed to show you have a flat belly. Which means *we* can't wear them," he adds, slapping his slightly convex stomach and chuckling, as a young man with a bare-midriff shirt and flat brown belly walks by us.

Moth Poem

HOW PAINED I was to hear an old friend so superciliously say, "If you really love him, you'll let him go." I was, long after the event, bitterly lamenting the loss of the beloved.

Yet, at night, when a moth, a dragonfly, a waterstrider, becomes trapped and frantic on my desk, I carefully capture it in my cupped hands, go out onto the back balcony (the moon is shining) and release it toward the light ... at last imbibing the wisdom of my friend's good counsel.

'. . . and then what?'

RENAUD CAMUS' *Tricks* proposes itself as purely a theatre of surface. I've just reread this undervalued work which appeared in English a few years ago. It consists of two dozen or so literal accounts of one-night stands. These *récits*, as I think they're called in French, give a bare minimum of the "scenery" necessary to make each episode intelligible. Usually, Camus meets someone to his taste in a gay bar, a bit of courting or cruising conversation is provided, the inevitable small problem of "your place or mine" is dealt with, and a graphic though not salacious report of the sex concludes the encounter.

But as well, tacked on to each "trick," in parentheses and set in italic type, is a little epilogue – the ". . . and then what happened?" Sometimes it is no more than a terse entry: "*(Never saw him again.)*"; at other times, a more elaborate explanation is called for, e.g.: "*(Seen again several times, but for five minutes, and always by accident. I interest him, he says, but not for the reasons which make him interesting to me. He'd like to have discussions with me. He gave me his telephone number. One night, when I called him, he was obviously making love. He declined the offer of my telephone number ('I know I won't use it, that's how I am') but urged me to telephone him again, which I won't do.)*"

What's more, from time to time, Camus gets into delightful compositional difficulties, necessitating additional parenthetical, italicized asides. For example, in the midst of writing "Trick XIV," about someone named Jean-Marc, dated June 7, he's forced to note: "*(Friday, June 30, three-thirty in the afternoon, I am falling farther and farther behind in this chronicle. Walter (Trick XVI) is taking a bath. I have been trying to convince him for two hours that I have to work, but first he wanted to make love again and turned me on without too much trouble, despite all my resolutions . . .)*" and so on. Of course, this inter-textual note acquires an additional filip of deliciousness – a moment when "the pleasure of the text" is truly fetishistic – by the fact that it introduces someone whose appearance in the text proper has not yet occurred – i.e., "Walter (Trick XVI)" in some strict logical sense *does not exist* – but whose presence is signalled, foreshadowed, even numbered.

This is not to discount the events of the surface whose presentation is charming enough. In fact, what particularly pleased me in these inconsequential *relations* leading to sex were the numerous conversations attempting to identify a regional accent or locate a certain provincial town.

> *"You know where Saint-Rambaud is?"*
> *"Saint-Rambaud . . . Wait a minute. That's near Lezoux, isn't it?"*
> *"Right, well, near – about fifteen kilometres."*
> *"A village on top of a hill?"*
> *"No, that's not it. It's down on the plain, near Pont-de-Dôre. You know Pont-de-Dôre?"*
> *"Yes, sure. I'm mixing it up with Beauregard-l'Evêque, for some reason . . ."*

It's the chit-chat that takes place on the walk from the bar to where the car is parked, after you've agreed to go to bed together. Indeed, it's exactly the sort of conversation I might (and in fact did) have in Vancouver with a young man from Sarnia, Ontario. Pornography is thus sabotaged by simple realism. The gay writer inevitably works on the edges of the pornographic genre, knowing full well that, from the outside, homosexuality itself is regarded as *a pornography*.

But what is it about precisely those epilogues, interruptions, asides, even moments on the surface, etc., that is so satisfying? Simply this: in a text that is programmatically superficial, they invoke, however casually, depths of being. The "tricks," by definition, argue a kind of anonymity of person; i.e., they appear in their role as objects of desire, which is to say, nonpersons; the epilogues insist on humanizing them by conceding their endurance beyond the recounted episode. Even the announcement of a disappearance – *"(Never saw him again.)"* – is a declaration that "he" nonetheless continues to exist, merely elsewhere.

If I were never to see B. again, I should have to conclude: *(Moved to Edmonton, where his sister lives. Occasionally, I telephone his friend Ian, who, tantalizingly enough, has just heard from B.)* Everywhere, intractable depths. Thus, the text declares that it is also so in "life."

The issue raised by *Tricks* or any similar work, it turns out, isn't only: . . . *and then what happened?*, but, as well, *what happened outside (beneath/alongside/beyond) the text?* It is as if a work should adopt the method of Andre Gide's *Counterfeiters* then, and provide a journal of itself.

à la *Tricks*

AT ABOUT one in the morning I spotted a solidly built blond-haired young man standing across the street in front of the cigar store on the corner of Polk and Sutter in San Francisco. It was the summer after we had heard about the plague. As I crossed the intersection, he walked down a couple of doors to the smoky plate glass window of a bar to comb his hair. Then he returned to stand next to me.

"What are you up to?"

"I'm up to five-feet-eleven," he joked lazily. He asked if I wanted sex and when I said I did we began walking south on Polk toward my motel. He wore a sheepskin-lined jacket, white wool pullover, jeans and boots. I noticed *through* the beauty of his shape the lines beginning to form around his stoned grey eyes. I judged him to be about 25, though he may have been younger, perhaps 22 or so. His name was Sean.

As we moved down the darker streets below Post, we agreed on a price. "Is it hard to get work here these days?" I asked.

"No, not really . . . You mean jobs or like on the streets?"

"Both."

"I can get a job anytime I want one," he claimed.

I was surprised. The night before on TV, the announcer, in reporting a local plant closure, had noted that the unemployment rate was in double digits. On the same program, there was a political commercial from a California gubernatorial candidate who promised to enforce the state's capital punishment law. "Is that so?" I asked.

"Well, not good jobs," he conceded. "You know, busboy."

I couldn't place his slight drawl. "You're not from here, are you?"

"No. From Sacramento," Sean said. I thought he was from further away, perhaps from someplace in the American South.

(In recounting all this later to George, a native-born Californian, he remarks sardonically, "Sacramento *is* the South.") I must have looked a little puzzled. "That's 90 miles from here," he explained.

"Yeah, I know. I drove through there this afternoon."

In the motel room he turned on the radio portion of the television and rolled a joint, sitting at the round worktable next to the bed. Kenny Rogers' "Back in Saigon" was on.

"Saigon," Sean said, naming the song. Then he asked, "Is that in Korea?"

"Huh?" I was startled. "No, Saigon's in Vietnam. You didn't know that?"

"I do now." He reached for my Zippo to light the joint. As we were getting a buzz, he remarked, "I don't like psychedelics." It was unusual to hear anyone mention hallucinogenics these days. I wondered if he had been frightened by a bad trip. "I got scared," he added, as if in answer to my unspoken question.

"What happened?"

"At first I had hallucinations."

"What did you see?"

"There were these, like, perfect illusions, you know, of knights in armour and all. Like knights of the round table." I noted his curious use of the word "illusions."

"What scared you?"

"I just felt sick and vomited and everything."

When I came out of the bathroom, Sean had taken off his clothes, except for his white gym socks. His naked, muscular body was stretched out on the bed. I stripped and lay down next to him. His beautiful torso was rather mutilated. In addition to a few small old scars on his belly and thigh, and possibly some track-marks, he had nearly a dozen tattoos, seemingly randomly placed, some of them elaborate and professional (a scaly dragon crawling down his bicep), others crudely amateurish.

The one that caught my eye was just above his bellybutton. It was either a sword or clenched fist, I can't remember which, with an arc of short parallel lines above it to symbolize the energy of the image. Below the fist were the letters "S.W.P." I put my finger on it.

"Superior White Power," he explained.

"What?" I asked, missing it the first time.

He repeated it. This time I heard it. It was too late to back out. And pointless to deliver a sermon. Instead, I again looked at the age-lines around his eyes and thought of the dozen or so haphazard occasions on which he had acquired these intended and unintended tattoos, marks and scars.

I caressed his cock. It was soft and slightly curved. When I moved closer to embrace him, I could feel his body resist. "I don't like kissing," he said. I backed off, moving my fingers across his sculpted chest.

"What do you like?"

"Getting blown . . . handjobs."

"O.K."

I went down on him, stroking his firm thighs and positioning myself between his legs. When his cock grew hard it tended to curve sharply up, flat against his belly. "Do you fuck?" I asked.

"Sometimes," he said, not too enthusiastically.

"Do you want to put this in me?" I asked, referring to his spit-glistening, erect, curved dick. He didn't.

"I guess you're unlucky tonight," he said.

"There'll be other nights," I replied, taking his cock in my hand. At least it meant I didn't have to get out of bed and go to the bathroom for rubbers. The radio played. Soon I could feel the cum swell through the hardness. It surged onto his belly, coating the "S.W.P." tattoo.

A couple of minutes later he asked, "Do you want to get off?" I had thought that jacking him off would be the end of it. I was resigned. There would be other nights, after all.

"You mean bring myself off?"

"Yeah."

The idea turned me on. I liked the thought of revealing myself to him while he lay there watching. I got up and got some K-Y and a towel from the bathroom, then laid down next to him and stroked my cock. Just before I came I rolled over on my belly and took his semi-flaccid damp cock in my hand.

Later, he stood in the bathroom, washing himself with a cloth. The door was open. The light in the bathroom high-lighted his firm, well-formed ass, powerful thighs, genitals.

He dressed and asked, "Is there a telephone in here?"

"There," I said, glancing at the pink plastic phone. He dialed information.

"Bus station," he said. He dialed the bus station, but the line was busy.

"Where you going?" I asked.

"Sacramento. I have the money for a ticket now. It's too cold to stay out tonight."

He dialed the bus station again. Still busy.

"Do you know what time it leaves?"

"There's one about two-thirty, I think," he said.

Just before he left he heard a familiar tune he liked playing on the radio. "Queen," he said, identifying the group, and turning up the volume. "It's a good song." But rather than stay to hear it himself, he said goodbye and left.

A few hours later, as the occasional car ground through the early morning hours before dawn, the imperfect illusion of Sean had faded from my mind. Probably he was on a Grey-hound, going to Sacramento.

(Never saw him again.)

On Condition

IN PARIS, long ago, a French boy my own age, about nineteen, a hustler, whom I had asked to sleep with me, replied, " . . . *par condition.*" I have ever since retained the sense in which all of life is presented to us "on condition." We slept together many times.

Eros

IT'S PROBABLY not a good idea to see either of them at their best. Blinding Eros; charming Cupid. Better to catch them off-guard, as they do us.

For an instant, they stand revealed in the merciless fluorescence of a public building, or their voices grasp at optic fibres. For instance, B., scruffy, unshaven, stoned to the eyeballs, making me drive him to the airport through rush-hour traffic, and then getting the flight info all wrong, forgetting his i.d., etc., so I have to use my credit cards for his fool's errand across the mountains. Or M., phoning collect in the middle of the night from some other time zone, with an incomprehensible tale of loss. So, one starts, and moans, as did Jack Spicer:

> *What have I gone to bed with all these years?*
> *What have I taken crying to my bed*
> *For love of me?*

But there is no denying how they marked us, broke our hearts, wrinkled our souls. One even left a blue anchor tattooed on my forearm.

THE FIRST TIME I saw B. was in the Ambassador pub. I can't remember the time of year, but it must have been sometime during the rainy season because it was pouring outside.

I cajoled my drinking crony Mr. Stevens, who had a special talent for such chores, to intercede on my behalf with a blond, curly haired sprite sitting several tables away. *Mister* Stevens was the camp name of this thin, fortyish man with pale, thinning hair and wire-rimmed glasses that corrected only about a third of his myopic sight. Because I was the member of our troupe most identifiable as "political," he liked to subject me to

Tory diatribes, the intensity of which were directly correlated to the level of alcohol in his blood.

I rather preferred Mr. Stevens' drunken and savage self-caricatures to his attacks on human equality. "Well, what am I?" he would wail, and then bathetically answer himself, "A third-rate hag in a fifth-rate faggot bar in a ninth-rate town." I appreciated in this the grain of half-truth that applied to all of us. In fact, we made a rather comic duo. Squinting behind inadequate spectacles at a hazy youthful shape, he'd ask, "How about that one?" It was like cruising with Mr. Magoo, the short-sighted cartoon character likely to mistake a tank for a toadstool. I felt like a seeing-eye dog reporting in, "No, not him."

He was not, however, without his redeeming features. Simone de Beauvoir once wrote, "Sometimes man seeks to find again upon the body of young boys the sandy shore, the velvet night, the scent of honeysuckle." Some nights in the bar, only Mr. Stevens could adequately verify this text by his rapturous description of teenage flesh – someone he had slept with the night before – as he ran his feathery fingers over my own forearm to illustrate his story.

Mr. Stevens returned alone from his mission, dropping into a vacant armchair alongside me at the terrycloth-covered circular table several of us were clustered around. "He'll be over in a minute," Mr. Stevens said.

This is perhaps the most tremulous moment in desire, equal even to the first sight of the desired one nude. The mildly entertaining or boring evening is about to go on without me. Lolo, heavy-lidded and magisterial, is grumbling his displeasure over Mr. Stevens and my lascivious gossip, his hopes for a literary turn in the conversation dashed. Mr. Stevens, by now, is listening to a plaintive anecdote by Ed T., an accountant. As Norman, the waiter, glides down the aisle with a trayful of beer, B. pulls up a chair at a tangent to our crude circle. On my lips the unimaginable yet utterly banal language which will cloak the arrangements for a startling intimacy. Equal even to the first touch; say, a hand placed around the curve of his side, just above the waist.

"LOOK, I'll be blunt," B. began, without preliminaries, but half-apologizing in advance for the commercial proposition he was about to make. I unhesitatingly agreed to the terms of the contract.

However, once we were out in the streets – we had quickly collected our things, made our farewells to our respective friends; "I'll call you," I yelled to Mr. Stevens, as if we were erotic scientists and I was promising to report my findings from the laboratory/bedroom – and had walked about a block and a half in the driving rain toward my parked car, B. surprised me by confessing he was too drunk, stoned or otherwise out of sorts for sex.

I was taken by his candor. Instead of our agreed-upon destination, B. requested a ride to the other side of town where he proposed to spend the night at a friend's house. Although this was something of a violation of the code governing such affairs – i.e., it suggested a relation based on respect – I acceded, having long ago been persuaded by my father's example that courtesy was a true virtue. In any case, I could enjoy the anticipation of our next meeting.

ALMOST NEEDLESS to say, even in such arranged circumstances, there is an element of seduction. At first, B. was a casual pleasure. That is, I became immediately unconscious of what had initially possessed me, Eros. But I sought to entice him, laying myself bare, openly admiring his evident charms, initiating a discourse of admissions. Soon he delighted me by the frankness of his expressions of pleasure.

B. was from a rural town upcountry. There was a monstrous but typical family: younger brothers in Prince George, alcoholic and physically dangerous father, a sister in Edmonton. B.'s sexual tastes were distinctly bifurcated. Presently, he was at the tail-end of a deteriorating relationship with a man in the suburbs, a salesman with whom, by B.'s own account, he had fallen in love – this casual acknowledgement itself opened a horizon.

Like many others his age, B. was living more or less by his wits and the welfare system. Capitalism, or more specifically, its disemployment of youth, rendered B. economically powerless. And as ridiculous as it often seemed, the world – or at least that part of it known as the media – was for the moment demanding of me an almost daily exercise of minor intellectual authority. I was called on, often at dawn, by the local radio station, for ceaseless commentary on a range of current issues, including the economy and the high rate of unemployment, especially among youth.

I'd have to be particularly obtuse – moreso than in my dimmer moments – not to recognize the inequities in class power between B. and myself. Worse, there's also, as it's known in Marxist argot, a cash nexus, which poses its own set of inescapable culpabilities, but I think I'll save that one for a rainier day. Nonetheless, as I began seeing B., I was struck by how the structure of the homoerotic tends to even out the standard imbalances in relationships – class, age, education, whatever. Partly, it is the forbidden character of this desire that accounts for its egalitarian current, that causes its relations to be fundamentally a collusion, a conspiracy, a project. But, more: in the sex of homosexuality, how often those who are, by definition, the dominated, become the dominant.

I'm not saying that homosexuality eradicates differences, just that it reshuffles the cards one is holding. It may seem as if I'm claiming some sort of superiority for gay relations and, perhaps – if somewhat sneakily – I am, but I also know better. I've seen enough heterosexualities that are sufficiently dense, tangled and constructed of sub-basements of charged feeling, that I'm little tempted to engage in a bidding war. Nonetheless, among the pleasures of that celebrated homoerotic sexual preference, then, are its *equalities, reciprocities, reversals*.

I once saw a movie called *Trading Places* – an update of the old prince and pauper fairy tale – with a boy named Michael. When it ended, as we were about to go home for sex, I suggested that we could "trade places" also. He was immediately enthused by this verbal play and the ease with which it could be enacted.

Similarly, the assumptions one makes about many stereotypical sex roles are often surprised by a reversal: one night in Numbers, a Davie Street gay bar, Mr. Stevens and I were taking pleasure in viewing the affectations of a faggoty but exceptionally pretty youth as he played up to various men in the room – "outrageous" gestures, poses, swoons. Yet, how often these effeminate youngsters startle us later in the evening with the certainty of their desire.

In sum, I succeeded in arousing a hitherto unexplored region – a utopia – of B.'s ardour. I can't say, I *gave* B. power. The very presumption is arrogantly self-defeating. The most that can be claimed of my volition is that I *enticed* us to an edge, or perhaps, since it all occurs within the boundaries of a code, I conducted us to, not a play-within-a-play, but rather, a reality-within-a-play, occurring within the sexual drama itself. Herein, a reversal which offers the possibility of counteracting the endemic will-to-possess. This also happens to be the key to sadomasochism: the apparent exaggeration of possession harbours the abandonment of the will-to-possess. In all this, for Sade as for Socrates, the consideration is ultimately moral, or else it is without interest.

B., from our first encounters, sought to diffuse the boundaries of the code, to make them ragged as a fjord, invoking ambiguous borders between coded and open relationships, in sex as well as within economic matters. In bed, one or the other of us "fully impaled," as pornographic purple prose has it, it was soon mutually obvious that we were engaged in "something more" than a protocol. And how often he transformed monetary transactions, for his own sake as much as mine, with the utterance, "You're helping me out," as though it was but a munificent loan whose return was not pressing.

41

The recurrent spatial metaphor for me is "beneath" – beneath the arena of the code, under the stairway, in the basement, where a friend and I, as adolescents, fantasized "initiating" another boy whom we desired.

However, just as I began to acquire the illusion, like Proust's Charlus, that my life would become considerably easier were B. to enter it on a more permanent basis, he announced a brief visit to his sister in Edmonton, which, instead, turned out to be a temporary disappearance.

WHEN B. phoned one crisp morning in early December – the beloved has the uncanny ability to announce himself or appear out of nowhere – I was in the backyard, seated on a kitchen chair in front of the Japanese plum tree, working (... well, pontificating) before a television camera, constituting myself as an imaginary being.

I hadn't seen him in three months. In the meantime I had discovered Buddy's, where I often brooded in contentment after a day's work on the book I was writing about local politics, and had even met a faggoty young man there with whom I was having an affair. The young man was one of those wonderful people from another planet, interested in clothes, haircuts, interior decoration – a devout reader of *Gentleman's Quarterly* – but who thought sex rather messy, sticky, smelly. In contrast, B. loved to get in and unpretentiously rut. Indeed, he appeared within the hour, stripped, announced his "horniness," which was formidably visible, and promptly, to paraphrase the Homeric poets, entangled me in his limbs. In the hazy enchantment of afternoon, the room grew languorous with smoke and recumbent flesh.

B. had changed, or certainly wanted to be seen by me, among others, as having changed. Nonetheless, it was his relatively unchanging "essence" that was of interest to me. He was at that naissance of adulthood when it seemed urgent that his identity become more comprehensible. He wanted to "get it together," as if he saw his life as a scattering of fragments that he now sought to gather into one place or link into a network. B. had returned to school and had decided, apparently, that there was a role for me in this scenario as unofficial tutor. To all this I found myself sympathetic, because it was B. of course, but perhaps also as a characteristic of getting older: increasingly, as I observed human striving from the minuscule distance of imagined immortality, it seemed to me that what people wanted was often reasonable, even modest. At the same time, the charnel-house of a society in which they sought to realize their ambitions appeared ever more appalling.

IN THOSE DAYS, not yet in love, I would arrive upstairs at Buddy's around 9:30 or so for our rendezvous. B. was already there, perhaps shooting pool with someone. There is an instant, seconds prior to greeting each other, which nurtures Eros. He is across the room, engrossed in triangulating a shot. I've just passed through a blur of men below. Like no other feeling, desire conveys with immediacy the *otherness* of the other person. He could be an utter stranger who happens to bear a pleasing resemblance to my favourite hockey player on TV.

In this pure glimpse preceding recognition, one also sees what might be called his other*li*ness. One afternoon B. and I agreed to meet in a straight pub not far from where he was living. He was having a beer with a friend when I arrived. The stripper had just come on and both of them were immersed in her act. I took a table some distance away to wait until it was over, casually observing B., seeing him not only as an other (so, too, am I, as Rimbaud celebratedly noted), but a degree beyond that in which there appears the chasm that separates everyone, in which would-be lovers see in the beloved, as if by foresight, the limited duration of their love, in which we see not merely otherness, which prompts us to respect the independence of his being, but otherliness, which tells us of the impossibility of knowing him, and a shudder passes through the body, echoing as the longing for "transparence." The stripper exits, and I approach; or B. misses a shot, and glances up from the table. For an even briefer microsecond, I'm thoroughly startled by beauty, as if I'd never known it before. Then we see each other. With a look, he lets me know the game will be over in a minute; he'll join me for a drink; we'll go home together.

FOR PERHAPS six months, I was in love with B. In a sense, I was almost the last to know. At first, I found myself mentioning B. to my intimates. I think this is more than casual, I'd say as casually as possible to my house-mate Lanny. Letters to George: B. carefully placed in a seemingly throw-away line. Or with Tom in the sauna, after a morning of racquetball, I'd obliquely hint that "something" was going on. "Maybe I'm a little infatuated," I told myself with the same innocent enthusiasm with which the Trojan horse was first greeted.

Then for several months I was subject to the *figures of love*, as they're sometimes called; at once, a continuous meditation, a constant reading of minuscule ambiguous signs, an incessant imaginary discourse about, with, directed toward, the beloved.

"The body makes for the source from which the mind is pierced by love ... So, when a man is pierced by the shafts of Venus, whether they are launched by a boy with graceful limbs or a woman radiating love from her whole body, he strives toward the source of the wound and craves to be united with it and to transmit something of his own substance from body to body. His speechless yearning is a presentiment of bliss" (Lucretius, *The Nature of Things*).

FAR FROM being blunt, as he had originally proclaimed, B. was evasive, Ariel-like, mercurial, moody, "hyper," panic-prone, goony. The capacity of youth for solipsism should not be underestimated. It was weeks, perhaps months, before it occurred to me that I was often but a character in an *internal* drama of his own, one which my own actions did not necessarily affect, variously appearing as wished-for-father, friend, trick/sugar daddy, sanctuary, "mature" man he liked/sexually desired.

ARRIVING HOME from work some afternoon I'd find B. in a T-shirt and cotton jogging sweats, listening to thunderous rock, having become horny. Raising his eyebrows, batting his lashes, in what looked like a parody of seductiveness but, I later realized, wasn't, he'd ask with a leer, "Do you wanna get fucked?" Yet, openness to the infinite degree is so rare among men that, despite the near-certainty with which he could expect my heartfelt "yes," I knew what it cost him to casually toss out that question, and was moved by the glee with which he shucked those baggy exercise pants to display the fine blond down of his thighs and hard cock toward which I inclined my head.

ON THE RECEIVING end, he urges me on, uttering confessions one would whisper only to God.

Afterwards, from across the room as he pulls up his jeans, B. says, "I needed that." Then unaffectedly adds, "Thanks."

"Really?" I ask.

"Yes."

IN BED, one night, B. suddenly cries out, "I no longer feel young." He is momentarily inconsolable over his loss.

OCCASIONALLY, I see him anew, through someone else's eyes. George and I arrive at my place. B. is curled up on the couch, watching TV, in three-quarters view, wearing only my kimono-like mock-velour robe (underneath, tan briefs). He turns to be introduced to George; involuntarily, I imagine I'm seeing him for the first time as George might see him. I'm struck by B.'s fragility, the way in which he resembles one of those delicate pale blue-and-white Chinese vases.

HIS INCONSTANCY: disappearances, journeys, imperative missions, casual fucks, an affair with a woman, instant friends acquired during drunken afternoons in the pubs. Erotic adventures that leave me breathless with lust when he recounts them: B. and a friend, Sticks (but I hear "Styx," the gloomy river between us and hell), are taken to dinner at a fashionable restaurant by three men, who afterwards suggest that all of them return to one of their houses. "It was supposed to be a party," B. says, "but *we* were the party." He shrugs at the inevitability of the ways of the world: B. blown three times in the course of the evening, and no doubt gives head in return ("but I told them I wouldn't get fucked"); Sticks fucked by all and sundry: "You should have seen him this morning; he was walking around bow-legged."

ENOUGH IDYLLS. Proust: Marcel "measured his pleasure in seeing him by the immensity of his desire to see him and by his grief at seeing him go; for he enjoyed his actual presence very little."

IT'S ALMOST OVER. I phone his former lover. He's seen B., who disappeared a week ago. The ex's cheery tones, my strained timbre. We're close to the last straw. I assemble the prosecutor's final summation: an imaginary speech studded with coolly delivered ultimatums, uttered in the tragicomic mode I learned while attending the medieval court of an early lover.

AROUND DAWN, a racket of crows, and then they fall silent. I wake desolate, having dreamt of B.

MEMORY: B.'s boast that the more he exposes of his body the easier it is to catch rides. Hitchhiking along the summer highway, clad only in gym shorts, a tiny knapsack at his calf. But one Sunday morning he phones in; I have to drive all the way up the Fraser Valley to rescue my stranded friend at a roadside restaurant. I'm touched by the thought that his beauty – so obvious it fairly cries out for notice with or without his efforts – is somehow invisible to almost everyone but me.

WEEKS LATER, after it's over, I'm in Buddy's with George, who's in town for the weekend. We make our way through the crowded bar, up the stairs, into an even denser pack of bodies.

Suddenly B. By the faint light of the cigarette machine, under the deafening music, jostled by passing forms, it is yet possible – our mouths in turn necessarily pushed close to each other's ear – to declare our mutual undiminished love. The crowd separates us. I'm with George and we're joined for a drink by the beguiling beauty, Michael. Past him, I see B. in the background.

AND AFTER we have exhausted these snapshots, how can we proclaim: This passed through me, like a torrent, staining the cells of my bloodstream ...?

IF I'M SHOCKED at the less than attractive sight of him (much later, in an airport), it is because Eros has left this body. The existence of the gods is immaterial; rather, they are a provisional answer to a mystery. Those in whom Eros once dwelled, now "sag a bit/As if five years had thickened on their flesh."

Cupid

FROM THE FIRST, I recognized Cupid, the god(let) presiding over crushes, infatuations, tricks, one-night stands, brief liaisons, and other lesser affairs of the heart.

He was stripped down to the minimum for hustling on a hot summer afternoon, sitting on a low stone wall in front of the church at the corner of Broughton and Pendrell, crossroads of the most notorious erotic zone in Vancouver's West End. For this incarnation, he appeared in brief cut-off jeans, white gym socks and runners. The rest was well-tanned, firm, nineteen-year-old flesh, on display for passing motorists.

The dazzling smile he flashed as I drove through the neighbourhood brought me back around the block where I parked opposite him beneath a pastel apartment tower. He crossed the street and leaned in through the car window. It was three o'clock in the afternoon. His name was M. We made a date to meet at a gay bar later that evening.

As usual, I was unprepared for fateful encounters. In fact, I carried the anticipation of M. as little more than a talisman to see me through the appointed rounds of a crowded day. Notwithstanding that our little corner of the globe is locally known as Lotusland, its citizens are, it must be admitted, a disputatious lot. It so happened we were once more in the midst of a familiar political crisis pitting the people against the state. We were about to take to the streets again, thus occasioning a familiar flurry of phone calls, committees, coalitions, and the gossip necessary to fuel such endeavours. When I met M., I was en route to one such assembly.

Nor was the temper of the present times the extent of my preoccupations. I'd lucked into a new teaching job, due to start in days, which required that I expound upon, among other things, ancient political thought. At the moment I was scrambling to augment my shaky understanding of the Roman republic, hardly expecting to run into one of its mischievous minor deities.

That night the August moon was at the top of Robson Street as I entered Neighbours, a raucous excuse of a bar, to find M. A mirrored globe slowly twirled over the dance floor, casting pieces of light across the men. From the crowd, I caught a glimpse of a busboy named Jason familiarly running his hand over M.'s ass as he passed behind him, and immediately knew that they were lovers.

The short-lived fashion of the season was khaki battle fatigues and other bits of jungle paraphernalia. M. wore a trendy military camouflage cap, leather jacket, blue T-shirt, and tight-ass jeans. "I have to peel'em off," he said, as he did so, once we were home. His white jockstrap – which he claimed to have donned solely to surprise me (needless to say, it succeeded) – glowed against his tanned groin. As his massive, uncut cock sprung hard out of the pouch, it didn't require remarkable foresight to intuit I was at the initiation of what might be more than a passing fancy. When I deep-throated him, a groan of pleasure echoed up from the bottom of M.'s throat.

AT BUDDY'S toga party a few nights later, M. arrived in the guise of a Roman slave, attired solely in sandals and a loin cloth, which was about the size of a pocket handkerchief. Most of the bar's patrons who had consented to go along with this outing contented themselves with laurel wreaths and pieces of bedsheet draped and pinned in the form of white togas. The prettier ones bared a summer-bronzed shoulder. Even the more priggish clientele who remained in civvies (myself included, alas) had to admit that the scene was delightful.

There was a prize for the best costume. It was destined for a gargantuan good-natured queen named Tiny who tended bar at a neighbouring establishment. He was decked out in the gear of a Roman centurion, complete with polished breastplate and crested helmet. M. was one of the contestants. The finalists formed a tableau on the little stage in the mainfloor bar as the M.C., one of Buddy's managers, imitating a TV game show host, maintained a bright patter while soliciting audience applause to determine the victor. When he got to M., the M.C. pretended to peer under his loin cloth, joking, "That's what pays the rent," as he flashed an exaggerated leer to the Roman mob. Stern faggotry, unyielding in its standards, refused, however, to award the triumph to mere Beauty; it favoured the centurion, on grounds of "artistic" merit.

As I stood in the white toga'd ranks of the condo gentry at this auction of the flesh, M. seemed to me heartbreakingly vulnerable in offering himself thus, subjected to public quips about his streetcorner activities. He, however, was indifferent to these indignities, apparently satisfied by the prior arrangement with management that his near-naked performance would be rewarded with an evening's free drinks, or perhaps content with the sighs elicited by the sight of his bare flesh, still warm with the day's sun, as he passed through the senatorial crowd.

CUPID, in addition to igniting the affairs of others, is himself, of course, constantly enamoured. It was a part of the old story I'd forgotten, or perhaps nobody had noticed before – Cupid carousing, having casual sex, stormily breaking up with his lover, discovering that all his boyfriends like him *too* much, etc. We only picture him presiding over our little tempests, forgetting he has a life of his own to disorder.

M. was lured by Jason's "butch *GQ*" looks (as he characterized them), though, I must admit, on the few occasions I ran into the object of M.'s affections, usually at Buddy's, I failed to appreciate the attraction. Rather, I instantly spotted Jason as a closet case, distrusting his hearty handshake and hail-fellow-well-met style.

On first sight and in public view, he had cupped M.'s butt in the hollow of his palm with the casualness of dominance or confident possession, but appearances, as usual, were deceiving. It was true that M. was in his most boyish phase, which often had a pleasantly effeminate aspect, even a touch of faggotiness – in contrast to Jason's studied manly ruggedness. Thus the fantasies of the voyeuristic chorus, consisting perhaps only of myself, imagined Jason driving his substantial dick (M. had already put in a good word for cock size) up M.'s ass.

But, in fact, as M. recounted it to me in a succession of nights that quickly stretched into the rainy season, their amorous games, which included a few scenes of mild bondage, weren't entirely predictable. It was Jason, although vigorously denying it even as he squirmed with his wrists tied behind him with a leather thong, who longed to be helplessly penetrated by his youthful partner, ejaculating simply from the combination of the friction of his cock against the sheets and the pressure on his prostate from M.'s well-timed thrusts into his asshole. Indeed, M. cleverly manipulated the situation to the point where he could issue ultimatums to Jason to bend over and take it. And Jason did, which seemed to me a rare point in his favour.

Naturally, such brutal intimacy could only contribute to the unsmooth course which true love must run. Jason resented M.'s working the streets, and responded with unfaithfulness in kind, barely troubling to disguise his adventures. Jason's preferred lubricant for sexual congress was Vaseline Intensive Care Lotion. One night, M. told me, he arrived home hot for Jason, wrenching his boyfriend's white jockeys from his hips, but even as he pressed forward to lick Jason's cock, his olfactory sense was assaulted by the smell of Vaseline Intensive Care, indisputable proof that Jason had earlier in the evening betrayed him with a rival from their handsome circle of friends, and then added insult to injury by not bothering to shower away the telltale evidence. It was that refusal to observe the protocols of deception that M. regarded as infuriatingly vulgar.

But then, M. was not exactly a paragon of monogamous virtue himself. First, of course, there was the business of hustling. Though Cupid is traditionally scorned for his cupidity, and it is true that he must make his way in the world, his behaviour is hardly, as his detractors would have it, a form of greed. M.'s views on hustling oscillated wildly, depending on the shaky state of his relationship with Jason. In his more maudlin moments – which, nonetheless, were rescued by his sincerity – he imagined himself and Jason living happily ever after in conjugal devotion, and vowed to abandon the street, sparing himself no recriminations for his whorish refusal to attain that blissful state. On less mopey occasions, M. admitted with an impish smile that, economics apart, he liked the "charge" hustling provided. Second, there was the possibility of erotic adventures of his own with members of the fraternity of his co-workers.

BUT WHAT of myself in this scheme of things? Especially since a friend notes, "Most will perforce identify your beautiful young men with 'whores,' and most men who 'go with' whores don't love them or want to hang around them." I had never thought of it that way.

When I was eighteen and in the navy, stationed outside Naples, I often went into town with the guys, where we hung out with the women at the Black Diamond Bar. Our foreignness exempted us from certain taboos of manliness – within whose code, for example, one was ordinarily shamed by "paying for it." Though I was mainly engrossed, even then, in barracks romances, and only infrequently sampled the pleasures at the Black Diamond, I was interested in those affairs between sailors and women which went beyond the terms of the contract. For both parties, there was something of a game – but also, more than a game. To cause such a woman to love you was considered a sign of ultimate sexual prowess. For her part, the object was matrimony. I noted that a law of averages appeared to regulate – and even ensure a modicum of "justice" in – the outcomes of these unconventional pairings.

My role model was Dooley, a wiry nineteen-year-old Boston Irishman. Never, then or later, have I seen such awe-inspiring purity of passion. In the middle of a desultory pinochle game in the barracks, Dooley would think of a woman he had seen in the Black Diamond, but had yet to sleep with. As Barthes notes, in a slightly different context, "Desire is no respecter of objects. When a hustler looked at A., A. read in his eyes not the desire for money but just desire – and he was moved by it." Dooley, rising from his chair, suddenly possessed, would conjure up this apparition before us, and then, gritting his teeth and lashing out an arm above his head at the end of which he would split the air with a snap of his bony fingers, cried out to his gods, "*Just one time!*" And he was off, making a dash for the last bus to Naples, leaving us to thumb through our guidebooks to the ancient Roman ruins of nearby Paestum.

But the prosaic and simple truth of the matter is that M., and the others, are persons. I saw him as a boy, as a young man. When you win his love, it is not the sex he loves, since he is already a past master of that, but *you* – for yourself, and for treating him as a human.

In any case, with M., I was caught up in the comic mechanics of desire. He wisely insisted on condoms, and soon I was in the drugstore, feeling exactly as I had at sixteen, confronting a vast display – made more confusing by the advances in technology that had taken place since my last shopping expedition – of "lubricated" and "regular," "ribbed" and smooth, "spermicidals," "snug-fitting," and a litany of brand names, such that you practically needed a degree in biology to buy a rubber.

What's more, I had momentarily discovered the secret of happiness, namely: life is imperative. The meeting begins in half an hour! I have a date with M. at 10! The notes for "Tricks" *must* be finished! I need more whipped cream for the chocolate mousse, *now*!

MEANWHILE, a seventeen-year-old hustler, oddly named L'Amour, or perhaps L'Amoreaux (I never did get it quite right, though I was later to know him), had developed a crush on M. Soon he was courting M. in that charming way younger boys have, bringing little presents to the streets where they waited for johns. M., wearing a silver chain around his neck that he'd received from this youth, and positively glowing, described in detail his enthusiastic deflowering of L'Amour, fucking him not once, but several times, thus perpetuating the myth of youth's relentless potency.

But what about Jason? I asked. M. shrugged helplessly, anticipating the impending domestic disaster. Cupid's genre, naturally, is bedroom farce. And since Cupid is the only immortal moved by boredom (a vastly underestimated emotion, as my friend George points out), inevitably L'Amour was introduced to Jason. The three of them were promptly cavorting in the same waterbed. My imagination reached a point of raw exhaustion. For a final twist, as M. and Jason quarrelled, L'Amour moved in with, of all people, Jason, testimony, once again, to Jason's unseen but nonetheless formidable powers. This was spitefully convenient for Jason, since he could revert to the dominant stereotype he preferred to identify with, now that M. was no longer around to hold up to him a mirror of his actual desire. Our mildly bereaved Cupid drowned his sorrows in the readily available libations and bodies, and bought tickets for – where else? – Christmas in Hawaii.

In all this, I'm affectionately bemused. After a string of debaucheries, M., nude, towelling off from a shower just before we head out for dinner and a movie, innocently announces, "I've got a lot of growing up to do." He squeezes by me on the way to his wardrobe, his flesh brushes my fingers, he tries on half a dozen tops, gazes in the full-length mirror, asks, "Do I look butch?"

THESE MOMENTS remain: one evening, M. amused me by casually glancing at one of those atrocious seventeenth century representations of Cupid which happened to be lying on my night table. Like someone complaining that a photograph of himself "doesn't look like me," he criticized its ugliness. "Yes," I readily agreed, "it doesn't do you justice."

OR: HE ASKED, more than once, if I might write about him. I was curious as to what advantage he saw. Well, just as letters are better than phone calls, he sensibly replied, the written word is preferable to memories. "You can read it again, you can *have* it," M. said. Votary of Cupid, his wish is my command.

AND THIS: we mate by candlelight. Its flicker throws the shadow of his erect cock, enlarged, upon the wall. Delighted, he points it out to me as I lay under him. The illusion of its enormity amuses him as he enters me and it disappears, giving way to the giant shadow of our conjoined bodies.

ON THE COLDEST full-moon night of the year, M. calls from Waikiki. He'd gone with a blond friend he knew from the streets, Skip, who now lived on one of the islands. The sole glimpse I'd gotten of this slim, faggoty, striking beauty one crowded night in Buddy's was sufficient to pique my interest. But it hadn't quite worked out. Though M. had planned to earn his way as he went, there apparently wasn't much demand in Honolulu for black-haired, native-looking, well-endowed nineteen year olds. The men thought blond Skip a more exotic sight. M. was lonely – for Jason, even though they'd split up, and he missed me and his friends at Buddy's. He even idly suggested that I might fly out. My temperamental caution, however, spared me that particular temptation of middle age, whose foolishness is quite distinct from that of young and old fools.

When M. returned early to rainy, cold British Columbia, he brought me a souvenir pineapple, and we resumed our sociable round of going to the movies – we preferred quasi-mythological tales of mermaids, Neanderthal men frozen in the ice, remakes of *Tarzan* – followed by dinners at Japanese restaurants, and sex by candlelight to the accompaniment of Pink Floyd and hashish. But he was pining for Jason, who was working at a winter resort in the Rockies. I empathized with M.'s lovesick condition, since I suspected I was coming down with a slight case of flu myself.

I went with M. to the shops in the underground mall where he picked out a beautiful sweater to take to Jason in Banff. "The amorous gift is sought out, selected and purchased in the greatest excitement ... we calculate whether this object will give pleasure, whether it will disappoint ... seem too 'important,' whether it will *perfectly* suit his desire" (Barthes). The box was encased in a special wrapping paper whose design consisted of Jason's name repeated endlessly, which M. could absently caress as the train took him into the Rockies.

Two weeks later M. calls from Edmonton in the middle of the night. I met him at the airport the next day. As one might have expected, it was a fiasco. Jason had met a young woman. I knew he was a desperate closet case from the moment I saw him. Not only are M.'s hopes rebuffed, but he is consigned to sleep on the sofa, while in the next room Jason beds down in comfort with his new enamorata. Nor does Jason refrain from pointing out to M. the advantages of social acceptability that accrue to him from this more conventional arrangement.

Of course, it doesn't end there. Resilient M. quickly acquires a new lover, a slim, muscular, mustachioed man in his mid-twenties with whom he'd had a brief previous fling. As usual, I fail to understand M.'s taste in lovers. This young businessman ran a frame shop with one of those cutesy names – "Frame of Reference," I think – thus providing M. with part-time employment and the opportunity to be built into his paramour's newly purchased condo. The man's only redeeming feature, apparently, was a rather terrifying and simultaneously thrilling piledriver/jackhammer style of fucking. But this virtue had little utility since M., in his mastery of Jason, had come to prefer being a "top."

Obviously, this affair on the rebound can't last. Indeed, by Valentine's Day, Cupid's own national holiday, M. and I were having dinner in Buddy's. M., seeking my professional advice as a writer, showed me the lengthy text of a proposed letter to Jason, offering him chance number 3,408. I savour the irony of being consulted on a Valentine composed by Cupid himself.

So it goes. But enough of infinite variations; let us hasten to the epilogue that assigns each one to his fate. Jason and M. tried it again, broke up, coupled, split. Eventually, Jason came to a deservedly cruel – well, not end, but – middle as the kept young man of a wealthy Californian and was last seen, stoned on cocaine, at the wheel of an expensive car, either in L.A. or New Orleans, imagining himself happy. As for Jason's short-lived girlfriend, she became friends with M., who once spent several days with her and her girlfriend in Montreal.

Notwithstanding my conceit of M. as Cupid, he was, of course, simply M. Which is to say, he was, in addition to his basically adorable self, the adopted child of an upstanding, Christian fundamentalist, monogamous, etc., Edmonton couple.

At various times, M. would lament, "I'm almost twenty and still a virgin," much to my astonishment that he would reserve that category for such quaint usage. At his worst, he would deliver a depressing programmatic speech filled with reactionary and repentent avowals. I think this was in the spring, after a ship's engineer with whom he occasionally tricked got M. a job aboard an icecutter in the Beaufort Sea, part of the Arctic drilling fleet based at Tuktoyaktuk, and just before he obtained a devoted new boyfriend named Kevin. He would give up his degenerate existence, avoid the fate of "lonely, old men sitting in gay bars," go to school, get married, have kids, attend church, the whole package. This, from someone who, just the other night it seemed, was causing men to drool as he pranced among them in the near-altogether. I could've wept. Happily, these declarations dissipated like a sudden squall at sea.

Nor was I forgotten in these dispensations. Fortune, Cupid's capricious cousin, occasionally smiled. For instance, M.'s friend from Hawaii, Skip, was passing through town, and M., amused by my smitten sighing, intervened on my behalf. Soon I was driving through the rainy streets to pick up this attractively fey blond – one of the perks, apparently, of moving in charmed circles.

FORTUNATELY, I fell in love with Cupid only briefly. M. had taken up with Kevin – once more I missed the erotic point of this choice, though I had to admit that the new boyfriend, who diligently held down two jobs as a waiter in the downtown hotels, was an improvement in character over those who had gone before. M. would return from a weekend romp with Kevin, triumphantly announcing, "We fucked our brains out," or, "we went through a whole box of rubbers."

I moped, either in person, or by mail when M. was at sea for his six-week stint. M. was quite gallant about it all. Once, when I was being particularly lachrymose at dinner, and he could barely conceal his annoyance, he gently pointed out that he was putting up with this ridiculous comportment only because it was me, and we were friends. When I received his letters signed, "I miss you and love you," and rather bitterly asked George, "What does that mean?", my guru replied, "It means he misses you and he loves you." This was confirmed by the ship's engineer who had gotten M. his job, an interesting, articulate man in his own right, who I eventually met in Buddy's and with whom I had avuncular conversations about our protégé. Alas, dejected lover though I momentarily was, it had to be admitted there was no flaw in M.'s affection. In contrast to Eros, Cupid's touch is light; rather than heart-breaking, the pain he inflicts but pricks the skin, almost as a reminder that the body is alive.

THOUGH WE are charmed by Cupid, it would be a sentimental mistake not to recognize his streak of less-than-well-intentioned mischief. According to legend, he empties his quiver under contract to Venus; in fact, he does considerable freelancing. Consider Cupid's geometry: M. is bored with his live-in boyfriend Kevin, and still wants to fool around with his ex-boyfriend Jason, so he brings in another hot number, Derek, to spend the night, though nothing overt occurs during the evening's party. As planned, M. groggily wakes up hungover on the morrow in an undulating waterbed to find Kevin and Derek getting it on. This provides a pretext to feign anger with Kevin for unfaithfulness – even though he was only going down on Derek in obedience to M.'s injunction to be less "clingy" – and simultaneously to deny he is angry. "Why should I be angry?" he ingenuously declares on the phone to a worried Kevin. Why indeed? He's already made a separate arrangement to see Derek. All of this to get Kevin disgusted enough to move out and thus permit M. to get it on in good conscience with Jason, who, unlike the predictable, faithful and loving Kevin, excites M. by being surprising, disloyal and aggressive. Naturally, none of these manoeuvres quite works out – pieces of a jigsaw puzzle that don't fit – and M. laments the human condition as he prepares to climb into bed with me.

Or, one rainy season, M. seems to be systematically seducing all my friends and former lovers. Since I'm already going with Pat, I can hardly complain. Soon, he's seen at the opera with my friend Tod. He's spent the night with Ron. Once, at 4:30 in the morning, Terry wakes me, needing a bed. "Well, climb in," I groan. "No, I've got someone with me," Terry says. "Who?" "M." Since they both have boyfriends at their respective homes, they need a place to fuck. And since it was raining, and they're half-pissed, they decided it would be nice to come over and drive me crazy. I suggest a threesome, a fantasy M. himself had conjured up several months ago, but now he wants Terry to himself. Actually, my proposal was quite innocent this time – I merely wanted to watch a master at work. Subsequently, I'm required to suffer M.'s sulky criticism of me for having failed to be a generous host, despite the fact that Terry proved not all that interesting to him, though the latter, on a separate occasion, offers a fairly enthusiastic account of having been ploughed by M.

FINALLY, some parting glances: M. has moved into a little ground-level suite in my neighbourhood, and has just disposed of his latest boyfriend, when I arrive to visit. Wrapped around his neck and torso is his latest acquisition, a two-metre boa constrictor. He shows me his fish-tank, which contains some colourful, swimming cannibals, and enthusiastically describes his intention to purchase a pet tarantula and, in fact, to assemble an entire bestiary, one of each phylum. I see M.'s boyfriends, sex partners, lovers, tricks, including me, as a *hominary*. One morning, he arrives at my place, just as Pat and I are getting up. Pat is in the bathroom, washing his face. M. has his snake under his shirt, its head and flicking tongue peeking up out of M.'s chest. He sneaks into the bathroom and stands behind Pat, who is facing the mirror. I hear Pat's yelp.

FRIENDS FOR about four, five years now, though we see each other less frequently, M. occasionally still drops by. Always in the latest style, he's wearing cyclist's skin-tight mid-thigh spandex shorts, and parks his mountain bike in the kitchen. He's rather bored with the young doctor he's living with in a fashionable False Creek condo. He picked up a seventeen-year-old innocent while riding in Stanley Park and introduced him to the sublime. There's a young man in his mid-twenties, but who "looks nineteen" and has a splendid ass and kinky habits. I feel my breath getting shorter. There are various oldies but goodies. He reels off their names. Plus, he has a videotape of one of his enemies masturbating, shot when the boy was seventeen, which M. is taking pleasure in showing around in revenge for various imaginary offences committed by said monster, who is very blond, very pretty, and very everything in his one on-screen performance. As long as the VCR is already on, we allow ourselves to be accompanied in our own ministrations by some imaginary beings practising porn on another planet.

LONG AFTER its haunting streetcorner figures have been dispersed to other districts of the city, its "property values" safely restored, the neighbourhood now cloaked in middle class tranquillity, I sometimes drive slowly through that place where I was first entranced by M.'s impish grin.

WHERE EROS cries out in his own desire, Cupid offers the enigmatic smile of the master of technique. Eros opens himself; the art of the lesser Roman deity is to place his pointed shafts well. Cupid is amused as his arrows are transmuted into our errors of affection.

I COME BACK to our Roman winter. Gruff Cato, worthy Cicero. All day I traced the doings of Pompey and Caesar in the last days of the Republic. Sure enough, as I'm having a drink at Buddy's that night, the air is afresh with rumours of return. Later, M. wakened me out of sleep, calling collect from Edmonton. The amorous existence is a matter of comings and goings. Again, it is time to meet him at the airport.

Amorous Despair

JUST ON the other side of the middle of my life I found myself, deep in the night, sleeping not in my body but in my corpse, still contorted with pain from my dying. Is it to evade this unspeakable terror that I've slid my palm along the inside of a thousand thighs? knowing full well that the habituating use of desire for this purpose would raise an insuperable barrier to the realm of love?

II
Discourse

God

FOR A WHILE, I decided to worship God. It was a god I arrived at through a method of logical deduction. If there is a God, what would he be like? I asked. He would be a real person in my life, I reasoned, adhering to a literally anthropomorphic view of the sacred. He would be beautiful and I would desire him. Since a friend of mine named Trevor had all those attributes, I concluded that Trev was God. Having settled on him, I then further deduced God's other characteristics from Trevor's behaviour. He was narcissistic, perplexed, rather dispassionate, flawed in various ways, etc. So was God.

At night I prayed to him by name. My entreaties seemed about as effective as other people's prayers to their Gods. And with Trev there was the added advantage that if my prayers failed to reach him, I could always phone. At least my religion was less aggressive and appropriative than that of those who declared, "I take Jesus Christ as my personal saviour." Did those baseball players I saw on TV, who crossed themselves before they stepped into the batter's box, really believe that God knew and cared whether or not they got a base hit?

Come to think of it, I found their all-knowing but perhaps not all-powerful God – since these praying ballplayers were often hitting around .220 – much less plausible than my modest, almost Grecian, choice of Trevor. When I tried to envision their God, all I saw was an old man sitting in front of a vast bank of television monitors. Somewhere between keeping an eye on the U.S.-Soviet arms negotiations and surveying the incomprehensible devastation of an earthquake in rural Italy or Yugoslavia, with homeless victims shrieking skyward, "Oh, God, what hast thou wrought?", he would presumably pause and say, "Hold it a sec, old so-and-so's just stepping into the box in L.A. in the eighth and I wanna see this single I'm giving him." Frankly, I prefer the God of Plato's *Parmenides*, who knows our world as little as we know his.

Certainly, accepting Trevor as my God didn't much affect our relationship. If I had said to him, "You're my God" – I can't remember if I did – Trev would have been merely bemused. Which is perfectly in character, since God is bemused by the worship he receives. Nonetheless, his appearances in my life stood up as well as the supernatural claims made for other deities.

Once, when I was feeling particularly bereft, Trevor and I were sharing a hotel room in Prince Rupert, a small coastal town in northwestern British Columbia seldom visited by God. I softly called out to him, "Do you want your cock sucked?" He was always rather ambiguous about my sexual requests. However, as in the case of the Greek gods, who regularly cruised and picked up mortals, there was no problem of inter-species sexuality. The Greeks, of course, stand in contrast to the authorized Christian god, whose one recorded instance of dalliance is presented with high seriousness as something of an exception, an "immaculate conception." "No," he replied in the darkness.

But a few minutes later Trev was standing in naked splendour at the foot of my bed. "What happened?" I asked. "I changed my mind," he answered with Olympian calm as he slid in beside me, proving once again that God's mind is unknowable.

Eventually, I stopped worshipping Trevor. Perhaps my need for God had evaporated. Trev and I nonetheless continued occasionally to go to Buddy's for a drink. I wonder if a baseball player, who, having renounced Christ's deity, would maintain His friendship. Would he, for example, continue to shag pop flies in the outfield hit by Our Lord?

Gay: A Tale of Faerie

ONCE, long ago, men said the word "gay" wistfully, ironically, with longing, invoking an elfin world among the trees; its denizens flit between the shadows; their sex, tricks of light. In that faraway, each act of it was made to appear a unique event, an invention, a revolt against nature. Its singers – teenage outlaws in the line of Orpheus – cried out: *"O, abnormale! O, abomination!"*, rescuing and cherishing each term of derision heaped upon them. Since their existence was denied, all communication between them censored, their practice punished, their history excluded, each one thought himself a white blackbird, exiled from everywhere.

Then the frog was kissed by a prince and the word "gay" released from its imprisoned form. Gay came out of the closet as a political declaration. "Gay is good," it was announced in the streets.

Within two or three years, a curious debate erupted almost uniformly throughout the discourse of "liberation." Although various names were given to the protagonists – "revolutionaries/reformers," etc. – they were, in fact, Utopians and Shopkeepers. In the course of their dreaming, Utopians invented androgyny, *égalité*, "the death of the family," critiques of romantic love, promiscuity, and aspects of sadomasochism. All these were but experiments, occasionally nightmarish, toward a utopian goal: a world in which no one thought of himself as a "homosexual" or a "heterosexual"; that is, transcendence of a binary opposition in the discourse of sexuality. The Shopkeepers, meanwhile, produced bombardier jackets, cockrings, disco music, civility and hanging plants.

Then they tried to turn gay into a "lifestyle," designed to legitimate homosexuality through commoditization and, as well, to commoditize the homoerotic. "We buy; how can we be bad if we buy?" gays asked Consumer America. At the same time, they sexually mass-produced what was once singular; nature was redefined as offering various options; homosexuality marketed as an "alternative" in a field of consumer "preferences." The mythic figure of this spectacle was the Clone: the replication of coiffures, moustaches, clothing fashions, physiques, tastes, ensures the standardization of desire. It works something like quality control procedures in manufacturing.

Sitting in a pleasant cafe having a cappuccino in the Castro district in San Francisco, I take in the apparition before me: on the one hand, the passing men out front and the sense of safety, pleasure I draw from them; appreciation of the attention to detail in the shops across the way – the famous "gay sensibility"; each suspended plant a Persian miniature of the Hanging Gardens of Babylon; or I imagine a boy arriving from any mean hinterland town, not having to suffer the furtiveness of a previous generation. Against this sanctuary: the ghetto; illusion that the ceaseless proclamation of the virtues of petty-bourgeois capitalism will "make everything all right"; reification of the phantasm "homosexual"; suspicion that constant cruising is a reduction of desire; group narcissism.

Then, a new twist for the times: a mysterious and fatal disease breaks out at the beginning of the eighties. "The poor homosexuals . . . have declared war upon nature, and now nature is exacting an awful retribution," trumpeted one of the early and more vicious commentaries, harbinger of things to come. In slightly more refined circles of bureaucracy – foot-dragging, indifference, studied ignorance. Under it all, repressed only temporarily, unmitigated hatred of men loving men.

At the mundane level: Warning flyers in the bars; "safe sex" guidelines; gays demand research money.

At the mythic level: Knights-errant, we enter the deserted and shuttered streets of the plague city.

In the Plague City

IN THE PLAGUE city, at 29th and Sanchez, a man is walking his dog.

THE PLAGUE: desire as terrorism; the body as a time bomb; cum as a bullet in Russian roulette.

ON CASTRO near Market, at noon, in the mid-day sun, abounding images of health prevail. In the plague city, a constant parade of men with sharply defined pecs, developed upper arms, washboard-muscled stomachs. Torsos encased in T-shirts, muscle shirts, tank-tops.

THE PLAGUE: epidemiologists plot exponential curves of infection; encampments of people living with AIDS settle in the UN Plaza under the flutter of rainbow pennants; the bereaved sew the names of the dead in a quilted register. I wake from an afternoon nap soaked in sweat, having seen my gangrenous leg blacken and rot.

IN THE PLAGUE city, the obituaries are delivered at "happy hour" by a lean blond youth in a black T-shirt with the word STUD in caps across his taut chest; his shades dangle from leashes as he heaves the bundles. We drink in Hunks at 5 p.m., checking the body-counts in the *Bay Area Reporter*. Its pages are crammed with eulogies, while outside, on Polk St., a passing bus bears the slogan: "AIDS – It's not who you are, it's what you do."

THE PLAGUE gives us the oxymoron of the year: "safe sex." Or someone is telling a story, and in the mere raising of an eyebrow we notice the periodization of sexual time, knowing that the events recounted occurred "Before AIDS." An apocalyptic instant shows me the "genocide" of a desire: as though watching one of those post-nuclear movies, like *A Boy And His Dog*, I imagine the extirpation of a thought from human consciousness, lost for a generation or so, having to be reinvented. The plague "cured" years ago, everyone inoculated, a teenage boy in a suburb (Terra Nova) wakes one morning thinking of a friend he saw naked in the high school locker room the other day, and feels a stirring, for which he has no words.

OF COURSE, the notion of "gay plague" was quickly and angrily rejected by us, and for good political reasons. But at the same time, is it not right to see the pestilence as plague? Thus we resist the panic, but do not avoid the horror.

AT SAINTS Peter and Paul in North Beach, where words from Dante's *Paradiso* are incised in stone, at evening mass "little candle-flames flickered helplessly in the reek of incense-breathing smoke; and with that cloying sacrificial smell another seemed to mingle – the odor of the sickened city" (Mann).

YET EVEN NOW, in the early gloom, a hustler cries out, from a darkened Polk St. doorway, mocking a dizzy queen: "Beat me, whip me, make me write bad cheques."

AT NIGHT in the plague city, troops of the dispossessed wander, their faces pebbled by radioactive grit; strewn garbage decays on the near-empty streets; dirt ground into the pavement so deeply you'd have to steam-clean the walks to make them sparkle again; yesterday's sports page is whipped from the curb by a chill wind; shadows gather in the columned porticos of public buildings along Van Ness.

SOUTH OF MARKET, on Folsom St., long ago it seems, we moved from room to room: Barracks, Ramrod, Stud. "There was much of the beautiful, much of the wanton, much of the bizarre, something of the terrible, and not a little of that which might have excited disgust. To and fro in the seven chambers there stalked, in fact, a multitude of dreams. And these – the dreams – writhed in and about, taking hue from the rooms, and causing the wild music of the orchestra to seem as the echo of their steps" (Poe).

IN THE PLAGUE city, almost morning again, trucks arrive with produce from the Valley, at Aquatic Park the 19 Muni bucks forward and grinds up Polk, the *Chronicle* is unfolded out in the Avenues.

AT 29TH AND SANCHEZ, a man is walking his dog. Now death takes its place as the organizer and the sublime of the community. If, perchance, I am not exempted – a possibility I'm not alone in imagining – the question that occurs to me is this: would I change anything I have said here about desire?

In the plague city, life goes on;
the sky clouds up; then it de-clouds.

Men Loving Men

IT'S REMEMBRANCE DAY. The movie columnist in the *Toronto Globe and Mail* is remembering a boy he knew in an Albuquerque high school gym; later dead in Vietnam; today his name etched on a black granite memorial wall among 50,000 others in Washington, D.C.

Also the frivolous: in *TV Guide* there is a pinup of the hot new actor in *Dallas*, denim jacket unbuttoned to the navel. I bestow a glance, allow myself a flash; daily micro-porn. But when I look under his cowboy hat, I remember B.

In the middle of an afternoon beer, as the Jolly Alderman pub fills with beefy jocks in club jackets, I'm explaining to the woman on my left why I prefer the all-male upstairs bar at Buddy's.

At which point George turns, and as if we were already in the middle of a discussion (which, in a sense, we always are), says: "I asked Lil: what is lesbianism?"

He continues: "She said: it's women loving women."

George goes on: "I said: I wish men had something like that, between gay and macho."

Immediately, I fall into the trap. "Well, what's gay, then?" I ask indignantly.

"Men chasing boys," George says without missing a beat, " . . . and macho is men chasing girls."

Later, he leans towards me, and confides consolingly, "Gay is also boys chasing men."

Possessive

I NOTICE a photo in *The Body Politic* of the winner of the "Buddy contest" held by Buddy's in Toronto. Although the identically named establishments in Vancouver, Toronto and wherever else are separately owned, the notion that the concept of a franchise exists in the world of desire lurks in the subtext. The victor is posed before the bar's logo in the place of the apostrophe, the sign of the possessive. I amuse myself by thinking that if this beautiful youth isn't at last giving the compulsion of possessiveness a good name, he's certainly putting a better face on it.

Types

DESIRE ORDERS itself with ruthless tyranny.

Mr. Stevens and I are waxing enthusiastic about a slim youth across the bar. Another friend chimes in with the offhand dismissal, "Oh, he's not my type." What is being invoked here? Or, whom do I exclude by this casual formula? I'm thinking of a young man I've seen dozens of nights in Buddy's: dark-haired, unobjectionably handsome facial features, a bubble-butt as he leans over the pool table, and frequent friendly greetings that might be read as an invitation. Yet, at best, I'm only half-attracted.

Which is to say, what is a "type"? And where does it have its origins?

Like others, I'm so accustomed to the presence of this self-imposed semi-conscious rule that it seems an abstraction, apart from myself, unassailable, a sphinx. Yet, its existence is not in question. Our friends have no trouble recognizing it. An acquaintance of mine, who's apparently "heterosexual," speaking about his older gay friend, admits with a smile, "I even know his type." Those close to me tolerantly put up with what my desire habitually seeks; it is a humorous foible, an endearing mania.

Even upon reflection, its explanation seems a mere banality. The type I'm attracted to is an idealized construction, or worse, a reproduction, a bad copy, of the image of one sought earlier (perhaps, or especially, unsuccessfully). And we're tempted to leave it at that. It is like an individualized fact of nature, *there*, resistant to examination, slightly embarrassing almost, an *image fixé*. The problem of types invites that current slogan which proclaims with a shrug the futility of discourse: "What can I say?" It, by its mere hold on us, seems to say it all.

"Well . . ." I often begin, refusing nullity, "can we not say
. . . ?"

FIRST, the prototype, whose image apparently continues to haunt us, is not an abstract "one," but is biographically specific: M., H., B., etc. As becomes immediately obvious: not one, but many (M., B. and so on): polytheism. Nor is there only one type: I can distinguish at least three.

This is not to deny that there can be an *Urliebe*, a first love, so imprinted that even now, in the squint of memory, I see the litheness of his nude body, Giacondan smile, ghost of light in his gray eyes.

We are alone amid the long wooden benches and rows of metal lockers, late afternoon, in the large steamy change room beneath or adjacent to the high school gym, having dawdled in the showers until everyone else had towelled off, dressed and left. In fact, the gym attendant caught us being last. Our "punishment" was to stay and clean up the shower area.

At issue, the touch – the one beyond the premeditated "accidental" scuffling whereby his cock is fleetingly brushed by my fingers; the touch – whose taboo we had so internalized by fourteen or fifteen that we knew its meanings would "identify" us (even if only to ourselves), perhaps irrevocably? For me: the manifestation of desire and the *birth* of homosexuality.

And an assertion: that there is a "birth of homosexuality" as opposed to the helpless conventionality, "I was born that way." For each one, then: a specific site, an other, a relation. If not a choice, at least an encounter, rather than a condition. Or, could we not say, in preference to a postulated genetic causation, that *it chose me*, "by a whole disposition of invisible screens, selective baffles . . ."? So, to speak of *an* aetiology of homosexuality or better, *homosexualities – pace* the stock cast of "domineering mothers," shadowy corrupters, *et al.* – is meaningless. It does not have *a* cause. Perhaps it is more appropriate to refer to each person's sexual *etymology*, rooted in events, persons, a specific geo-political milieu. I wouldn't be surprised if this principle of specificity also held for male *heterosexualities*.

WHAT'S MORE, the typology fails to obey a single set of rules or constructive principles. I'm attracted to the type embracing A., F., R., by the hawk-like shape of their noses. For others: curly blond hair; bare upper arms from boyhood; wide, sensuous mouths (M.). Whereas the type focused around H. (one adolescent summer in Chicago) seems to have as the source of its excitation the social fact of his potentially menacing otherness, or is it "straightness"?, yet his physical features might often be described as possessing a delicate prettiness. A third type draws me solely by the demeanour of his beauty, an almost virginal disposition, as if his consideration of me was a priori to any sexual preference. One of the first things I said to a future beloved upon meeting him was, "Do you want to fuck?", expecting that the outrageousness of this remark, delivered as a parody of a come-on, would protect me. I was startled to look up into his blue eyes and find that he was pondering this proposal as a simple unaggressive interrogative.

Perhaps, I think, a map will make it clearer:

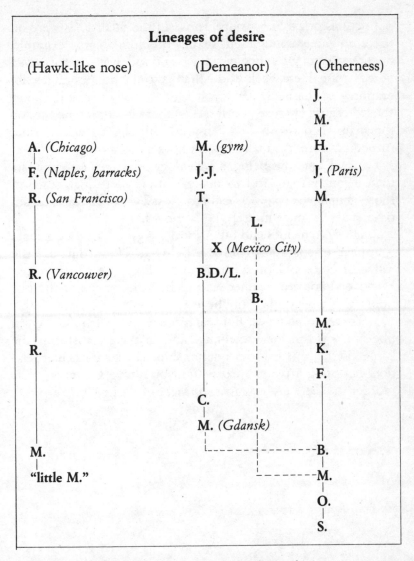

Lineages of desire

(Hawk-like nose)	(Demeanor)	(Otherness)
		J.
		M.
A. *(Chicago)*	M. *(gym)*	H.
F. *(Naples, barracks)*	J.-J.	J. *(Paris)*
R. *(San Francisco)*	T.	M.
	L.	
	X *(Mexico City)*	
R. *(Vancouver)*	B.D./L.	
	B.	
		M.
R.		K.
		F.
	C.	
	M. *(Gdansk)*	
M.		B.
"little M."		M.
		O.
		S.

From which I draw these provisional conclusions:

1. As cartographer, I began by thinking there were three types, terms, continents. But in the mapmaking, I discover more. For example, there appears to be a fourth type (indicated by the broken line), constituted, as far as I can tell, by a

politico-historical dimension. Those in the other lines were often ambiguous about their sexual preferences: for example, one lover, a tough Vancouver East End kid, was hetero/*sexual-homo*/erotic. Here, each was – thanks to the politics of gay liberation – unabashedly gay, or at least sexually available almost solely because of those politics. And there is a fifth type (not on the map): Scots-Irish, reddish-gold hair, light freckled skin, turned-up nose. And who knows how many more?

For each amorous being, a genealogy of desire more intimate than a family tree. And to make matters more real, some of those in one type (B., M.) begin to cross over to another. As another scientist once muttered, "It moves."

2. How often cities and other locales – gym, barracks, a room – appear inseparable from the beloved. How romantic the range of cities as I press them to my lips. The streets, cafes, *routes* of Paris are retained as much as the image of the boy upon whose belly I laid my head.

3. There are no types. For, each successive person in a given line is known in his specificity, and in turn, transforms the "type" in the course of our relationship. Thus, a particular relation can bring a type to extinction, or submerge, mute, blur, reorder it. There are, at most, *lineages* of desire.

Personals

READING THE sex ads in gay newspapers and magazines, I quickly become giddy with the multiplicity of possibilities. If the personals propose a bizarre funhouse (complete with distorting mirrors), they also conjure up a horrific vision of the kind portrayed by Bosch or Brueghel: an immense landscape seething with "tops," "bottoms," "b.j.'s," "j.o." circles, flagellations, spankings, copious showers of urine, and a litter of paraphernalia: jockstraps, dildos, enormous machines ramming all orifices. Column after column of listings, they offer countless testimonies to the pluralism of desire.

For the most part, they're organized by geographic unit (Indiana, Kentucky, Louisiana . . .), but couldn't they, I wonder, equally well be structured according to sex acts desired, type sought, age differentials, whatever? A similar thought, if it hasn't already, will soon cross the mind of a software designer.

The literary problem the sex ads pose to their authors is the material constraint of having to condense one's exfoliating desire into an identifiable shorthand. The result is a density of abbreviations, contractions, phoneticizations. Perusing them, I feel like a member of the Erotic Intelligence Corps engaged in cryptographic decoding somewhere in a sub-basement of the thousand-year Battle of the Sexes.

Ironically, some of the personals are utterly impersonal:

> . . . Gr p, Fr a/p, seeks man 18-45
> must be extra long & thick – looks
> & personality unimportant – must be
> heavy hung. Send photo & letter &
> size to . . .

"Looks and personality unimportant"? Does he really mean

that? What if a large, grouchy ape equipped with the requisite banana-sized genitalia turns up at his suburban door?

Or, what do you make of this? Here's the entire succinct text:

Plug my hole. (Area code 212) 989-3252

At least it's cheerfully non-discriminatory, free of those "no fats, fems, or blacks" strictures one often encounters.

Here's one from the appearances-are-deceiving department. An apparently gay white male is looking for another gay male, but describes himself as, and insists that his partner also be:

strt-actg, strt-appr

You don't suppose all those hundreds of thousands of "straight-acting, straight-appearing" men out there, sewing up business deals, jack-hammering the pavement, shooting each other in faceless deserts, etc., are really . . . ? I mean, why did we invent homosexuality, anyway?

Then there are those people, not satisfied with having one of themselves, who insistently "seek same," as in:

Happy sexy man would like to meet same . . .

or

*G/w/m, married, wants to hear from
similar over 30 . . .*

I look forward to a follow-up ad from a narcissist having discovered the error of his ways. It might read:

*Last week sought "same." Found him.
Now seeking "opposite."*

Certain appeals seem to be from victims of vocational misplacement:

*I want prolonged sessions with willing,
submissive students 18 + who are sexually*

eager. Permit playful pain to pervert any
vestige of virginity or youthful innocence ...

Why didn't this correspondent simply go into college teaching
if he wanted "prolonged sessions with willing, submissive
students 18 + "?

A number of entreaties come straight from the combat zone:

> *Slow Torture*
> *training. Potential POW, 32, 6'3", 185#,*
> *looking to learn his true limits from a*
> *hard-mscle Marine tough enuf to take me*
> *hand-to-hand, rough enuf to see to it I*
> *get* ... *etc. Pref outdoors – the more real,*
> *the better.*

Must be from an American serviceman seeking reassignment
to Beirut.

Of course, in the era of AIDS, these self-characterizations
are invariably accompanied by the reassurance that the author
is "health conscious." That may mean anything whatsoever.
The correspondent perhaps ate a handful of chewable Vitamin
C tablets this morning, or maybe he's a full-fledged hypochon-
driac.

Throughout, I vacillate, both in poring over the texts as
reader, and in writing about them. On the one hand, they call
forth a gently mocking light journalism; on the other, and
equally, they invite Talmudic commentary. Is the

> *Respectable group in X county now forming*
> *j/o club for regular meetings*

only for fastidious folks who prefer not to jack off in the com-
pany of ne'er-do-wells, deadbeats and other suspicious types?
When the

> *Hairy, muscular g/w/m, 32, 6', 160#,*
> *seeks comely, hairless guy (18 +)* ...

does he recall the post-Chaucerian citation: "No comlyar creatur of goddes creacyon"?

Collectively, the personals provoke a mirth beyond moral judgment, each succeeding appeal more excessive, elaborate, compulsive than the last. Yet, just as I'm about to be borne away on a rising stream of bubbly giggles, the oracle of desire itself stops me. It declares, these are lost souls trying to figure out how to reach each other. I catch myself also looking for a form inhabited by Eros. He would announce himself thus:

> *Thoughtful ephebe, 18, searching for*
> *ancient philosopher to educate and/or*
> *corrupt me.*

Perhaps he'll have a sense of humour, I think.

After shouldering past shades demanding "1-on-1" relationships – are there other, more athletic formations? – or noting that "handballing" has become the preferred euphemism for "fistfucking," or seeing the phrase "water sports" and imagining water polo players cavorting in a swimming pool, only to catch myself up short by recalling that "water sports" refers to pissing on someone, finally I find somebody who sounds just like me:

> *I am a successful writer, middle-aged. I*
> *live in my own home, and I smoke and drink*
> *moderately. I like the theatre, some concerts,*
> *movies, good restaurant dinners, but some*
> *nights I enjoy just watching TV ... etc.*

Clearly, too good to be true. And anyway, I'm not looking for someone just like me.

But inevitably, we must imagine the personal ad we would place on our own behalf. Facing the vast Gomorran plain of print in which all these lusts, longings and loathings are being simultaneously expressed, I abandon myself to that form of mild despair known as whimsy:

Cowardly literary lion seeks frisky
semi-literate lamb to lie down with.

All this, as Robin Blaser says, in pursuit of "the comical physical union our arms like briars are wrapped around."

Implicated

AN ENTICINGLY pretty youth crosses the path of Billy, one of the pool-playing regulars at Buddy's, who is sitting on the bench behind the felt-covered table along the west wall. As he reaches up, stretching across Billy's seated form to scrawl his name on the chalkboard, some remark in their obviously playful banter, which I'm unable to hear, inspires Billy to suddenly and sharply slap the very spankable bum at hand. The sting of it causes the boy's torso to reflexively arch like a cat's. He flicks his curly head in Billy's direction, hissing out a taunt or dare which formally threatens reprisal but in fact invites a repetition to which Billy, now half-rising from his sitting position, responds by smacking the kid's bottom again, just as smartly as before. And perhaps – this time both of them standing, Billy's rooster-proud body taut with excitation – there is a third occurrence, played under the rhetorical figure of "this time you've gone too far," in which the boy's forceful but feigned objection provokes another well-placed swat across his rounded butt.

This micro-scene of extraordinary intimacy takes place in the space of fifteen seconds or less. It remains unknown whether in the course of it, the lovely tempter is further inflamed by a fantasy, or even whether he'll later masturbate over a sequence of images, in which the two of them are stripped, the roles of obeisance and mastery even more precisely demarcated, and the actions infinitely repeated. Nor is it known what occurs in Billy's mind. As quickly as it happened is it dissolved, yielding a placid normality as Billy moves to attend to the game before him, and the boy, with a casually affectionate farewell, steps in the direction of another boy he had been publicly cuddling with moments earlier.

Now, no matter how much I should like to distance myself

from the implications of my arousal at the sight of this apparition, evade the uneasy set of complicit pairs (s/m, pain/plea-
sure, submission/domination, worshipper/adored . . .), or offer
reasoned protest against any eroticization of power – in short,
however much I recoil, I must recognize the surge of un-
reasoned feeling that rushes through me at that moment.

Lost and Found

IT'S THE LOSS of the momentary that overwhelms me. Not that of the long-held and deeply loved. For instance, in the supermarket today, I see a blond-haired young man. The appearance of his beauty is so startling I want to call him a "creature," as though he transcended species boundaries. He's deliciously long-legged, wearing maroon shorts made of an odd soft fabric like worn terrycloth, an unbuttoned shirt showing a frail chest, flat belly, and in his ear, a tiny gender-unsettling gold button. I am, for a moment, both entranced and aroused. Then he's gone, aboard a bike, grocery bag in arm. And even as I strain for a last glimpse of him from my trapped place in the checkout line, immediately a remorse creeps upon me with the knowledge that I shall likely never set eyes on him again.

On the late-night news, in the midst of a desultory item on pesticide poisoning – a familiar reporter is unsuccessfully attempting an interview along a semi-rural suburban roadside – a blond boy, mid-teens, in jogging shorts, bare-torso, suddenly lopes across the screen. A moment later – cut to close-up of interrogation of suspected polluter – the boy appears again in the background as a bystander. He is so extraordinary as to wrench a cry from my startled throat.

In Numbers one night, Terry, age 21, slightly drunk, describes, in his unaffected way, a seventeen-year-old boy he had recently encountered – blond, perfectly formed, huge dick – whose beauty was so astonishing as to even excite Terry himself. "Did you have sex with him?" "No, he was Larry's lover." I'm delighted by the innocent enthusiasm of Terry's praise of beauty and his lack of envy about the size of the other boy's cock. "Where did you see him?" "He was coming out of the shower. It was *big*." I imagine an apartment where such intimacy might be possible, an architecture containing Terry, the boy, their respective lovers. For an instant I fall into despair, grieved that I'll never see this ephebic god . . . such is the vastness of the world.

The fallacy, in each case, is contained in conceiving of his appearance/disappearance as a "loss," thereby implying "possession." If only I had developed the temperament that would regard his brief presence as a "find," then I would still "have" him.

Anal Sex

AT FIRST GLANCE, it appears impossible.

The asshole is an opening, unlike the mouth or eyes, almost entirely devoted to being closed. Whole cultures constitute themselves around the training of its "self-control," its sublimation. "The anus is the first organ to be privatised, to be excluded from the social field" (cited in Guy Hocquenghem's *Homosexual Desire*). Furthermore, and again unlike the mouth, which both takes in and emits a variety of substances – food, language, fire, breath, spit – the asshole's activity is officially unidirectional; unifunctional, in contrast to the penis. To get fucked in the ass is to radically reverse its course, its nature; nature itself.

Touching, mutual masturbation, perhaps even cocksucking, can be accommodated in the half-dare/half-playfair boyish discourse whose slogan is, "I will if you will." Whereas, the acceptance by males of anal penetration is an inescapable confession of desire – abandonment of heterosexual manhood.

In one pornographic novel I read, though both boys have sucked each other's cock, once one boy has fucked the other, he says accusingly, "You liked it; you're a fairy." When the other plaintively retorts, "But you liked it too," the first dismisses him out of hand: "I know what it is to you. It doesn't mean that for me. You're queer."

Historically, no sexual act has more excited legal outrage. Before prohibitions against homosexuality, the authorities forbade buggery, irrespective of sex or species. Unspeakable sodomy sends a frisson echoing down the spine of well-ordered society.

"Homosexual desire challenges anality-sublimation because it restores the desiring use of the anus" (Hocquenghem). Beyond the abandonment of "manhood," it is homosexuality's means of access to the loss of identity. "It is no longer I who am speaking when the desiring use of the anus asserts itself" (*Ibid.*).

Here: all the oscillations of the eroticization of power. R., having agreed to take it, nonetheless trembles at having "to play the woman's role." Herein: a moment of truth – the intimacy of B., the gargantuan size of S. Here: the most extravagant of gifts. M. turns over to let me fuck him for the first time since we started having sex. He declares: "It was the only way I could think of to let you know you're really special."

Mostly though, I bow down naked before him, somewhat in the Japanese manner, although I'm facing away, thoroughly obeisant, awaiting his pleasure, and mine too. "Who is saluting whom?" Barthes asks.

In the dog-years of the plague, this act portends ultimate risks. We know it to be the principal route of transmission of a deadly virus. For those who nonetheless choose it, a ritual of "playing carefully" becomes *de rigeur*. M. deftly unrolls the latex down his thick shaft.

During the brief period of the initial penetration, anywhere from 30 seconds to a minute or a lifetime: invariably, the terror and thrill of surrendering the will-to-possess. Sometimes M. teases – his condom-sheathed cock just inside me – with short, rapid, tantalizing thrusts, so that the anus must dilate and "reach out" to him, display its willingness to abandon the will-to-possess; then, slowly, inexorably, he takes possession; then, I abandon *myself*, I am his.

In Memoriam (Variations)

I

SHOULD MY cursed name slip from your lips, take solace in knowing I did not cheat the nets of being. In my stumbling, the lurid illusion of beauty rooted in the human form left me bereft a thousand nights. I was plagued by the melancholy of my race and, often as not, my senses were dulled. Why isn't love as great as it should be? I asked, in imitation of Jack Spicer. No human voice replied.

Let my enemies relish the spectacle of my ridiculous pomposity reduced to weeping. Where was I when I stared into the horror? The alabaster and indifferent beauty was barely scenic recompense while, on stiffened knees, bored beyond belief, unable to breach even the shield of fantasy in this parody of sex, I half-gagged on his acrid discharge, and the stale odour of desire clogged my nostrils as I gazed into the unblinking eye of mortality, sickened unto death by the fate I had so bitterly resisted to no avail.

II

WHEN YOU come to consider me, do not unduly grieve. Rather, consider this: along the way, I carried an image of beauty rooted in transient human form which the suffering world permitted me to honour a thousand-fold. I was blessed with my father's courtesy, and moments of attentiveness. Such fortune allowed me glimpses that Love is True, as my friend George puts it. What more could one wish amidst life's turmoil?

My good friends will remember my ready laughter. Where was I when I was seeing the comedy? The golden youth was happily on his belly, and I between his legs, his wondrous genital peeking from his splayed scrotum, its head between my lips while my hands roamed the globes of his butt, my flared nostrils catching the delicate scent of the peach-feathered birds of China as I gazed into the crystal-ball eye of the cosmos, deeply amused by the fate I had long since taken to heart.

Travelogue

I LIKE the way George resists, either with a word or by a gesture of indifference, announcements of sexual exploits ("I slept with so-and-so last night") unless, that is, the teller can provide details specific, tender and penetrating enough to render the event singular and, thus, of interest. Which is to say, George demands of narrated erotic adventures the same standard of intellectual or literary quality he requires of political ideas, poems or good travel writing.

Homosexual/Heterosexual (The Ideology of Sex)

GEORGE IMAGINES a logosphere in which the ideologically charged pair, *homosexual/heterosexual*, will be no more significant, or worthy of attention than, say, *horizontal/vertical*.

In fact, my distraught friend, just slightly inebriated, is yelling over the music at about one in the morning as we're seated at a table on the main floor of Buddy's, a table which he is rather violently shaking – a prophet possessed – to emphasize his point: "There's no 'homosexual'! There's no 'heterosexual'!"

Meanwhile, I, with my cringing middle class manners, and distracted from covert cruising, am dreading a "scene." Didn't my mother warn me about associating with the unpredictable Irish, or perhaps it was, more generically, simply the *goyim*? The determining binary categories of my early adolescence were *Irish/Jew*, an always potentially violent and, for me, semi-erotic set of opposites. Although she couldn't have known it, my mother was referring to the Murphys, two of whose three teenage sons I was at the time enamoured of. They lived under the navy gray wooden backporches in a basement hovel which, astonishingly enough, had or was rumoured to have a hard-packed dirt floor, as if in the midst of a twentieth-century working class neighbourhood an encampment of Neanderthals had squatted. Through the open cave door I had glimpsed one of them in the near-darkness, leggily attired in no more than white jockey shorts, thus seizing forever upon my pubescent imagination, linking desire with a notion of the *primitive*.

Come to think of it, how unprejudiced my desires were, as I indiscriminately loved not only Irish and Jews, but Greeks, blond Protestants, ebony youths. In the gymnasium changing room, I always contrived to pick a locker next to Randy, a beautiful black teenager. My whole aim was to ensure myself the pleasure, both at the beginning and end of the period, of seeing him naked as he stood on the wooden bench in front of the metal cubicles and watching him step into or out of his jockstrap while I, seated at his feet, both in fact and metaphorically, surreptitiously glanced upward into his groin, perhaps microscopically inching toward him in response to an imaginary "crowding" and jostling from others, in the hope that his limber and gleaming cock might accidentally brush my hair. It was an adoration so "subtextually" obvious that I even have a vague recollection that he once gently mocked our proximity by thrusting his genital toward my face. I must have responded with held-in embarrassment and fear, but I was also secretly satisfied that my longing had been recognized. All of this was at the time of informally enforced segregation in "mixed" high schools, such that any contact between students of different races was thought suspect. Sexual contact might still have been thought impossible.

Yet, even as George is vociferously protesting on behalf of sexual nominalism, I can't help but notice that we're in a place whose very existence is predicated upon one-half of this antinomy. Nor does the irony escape George, who goes on, "*This*, with all due respect to the humanity of the people here, is the perpetuation of a nightmare." He's referring, I take it, not only to the reifications sponsored by such an establishment – that is, to enter a "gay bar" you have to perform a matching mental exercise of identifying yourself as gay or not-gay. But also, George is pointing to its obsessiveness. The preoccupation with sexual discourse encouraged here trivializes the possibility of conversation. And, as well, George cites its irresponsibility: "A party every night," promises Buddy's drink coasters. "By the way," he adds, suddenly, and no doubt to mollify me, "this is really a great bar."

THIS "THEORIZATION," whose recorder I'm destined to become, is no mere outburst of a single agitated evening but, as is characteristic of conversation among my friends, an elaborated thematic played out over months, a year, until it defines a discourse.

On another occasion George expounds his objections to the *homosexual/heterosexual* dichotomy schematically:

1. It is obsessional or fetishistic because it defines people by their "so-called sexuality," an unwarranted attention to a single facet of being, and conversely, an unjustified exclusion of other and no doubt multiple and equally significant features of a person. That is, such usage distorts, as does any reductionism.

2. Even in itself, it is simplistic to assign this rigid binary opposition as a definition of erotic preference because people's sexualities are in fact far more complicated. For example, what do you make of this? For Pat, a friend of mine, one of his most important sexual preferences is what I would call "parasexuality"; that is, he appears to prefer sex "side by side" with his best friend, Fraser, and some third party, who may be, indiscriminately, male or female.

3. It is unscientific: as a linguistic practice it offers no evidence, à la Kinsey, say, to support these terms.

4. Finally, its usage is punitive or ideological, which is to say, rather than explicating or illuminating reality, its utterance is meant to carry a weight of disapproval or, at the least, enforcement.

Summed up: "*Homosexual* and *heterosexual* are inadequate terms to describe human beings. That's the main idea," says George.

THE HISTORY of these two lexical items, only recently conjoined to become a pair, ought to disabuse us of the illusion that the disjunction *homosexual/heterosexual* exists objectively outside of language.

The term "homosexual" takes precedence. It makes its first appearance in English in John Addington Symonds' *A Problem in Modern Ethics* (1891) and then, in the work of sexologist Havelock Ellis (who complains of the word's barbarism, constructed as it is of one Greek and one Latin stem), with the meaning (in the *Oxford English Dictionary*) "having a sexual propensity for persons of one's own sex."

The midwives to this neologism were themselves practitioners of the art in many cases, a fact which is evidence enough of an ideological strategy to transfer the description of homosexual phenomena from the discourses of morality and criminality to those of psychology and anthropology. The invention of "homosexual" or other, now-extinct terms, such as "invert" and "Uranian," then, is a linguistic act with implications of political advocacy. Of course, the passage from "sodomite" to "homosexual" did not exempt those so designated from social retribution. And, while the medical model obviates the need for clerical intervention, it makes the condition liable to clinical investigation. By the mid-twentieth century this phantasm is attended by a vocabulary which speaks of its secret existence ("latency"), recognizes its "symptoms," and projects its course of development: once past a "normal adolescent phase" it becomes a "disorder" or "perversion."

Not until 1901 does the counterpart to "homosexual" make an appearance. In Dorland's *Medical Dictionary*, "heterosexual" was defined with unconscious poetic justice as "abnormal or perverted appetite toward the opposite sex." Some would say that under tyrannical patriarchy, there is a sense in which all male heterosexuality is a "perverted appetite."

But apart from this accidental appearance in the frenzied "scientization" of sexuality, "heterosexual" is so sure of itself, so hegemonic, that it can disdain specification. So in various dictionaries through the 1930s and '40s, one searches in vain for this entry. Of course, heterosexual has a much longer colloquial pedigree – George performs part of a 1930s Noel Coward song for me that includes the rhyme: *"I'm an intellectual/I'm a heterosexual."* But not until the 1955 addenda to the third edition of the OED is *heterosexual* again required to officially define itself and, even then, does so in blatantly ideological language as "pertaining to or characterized by the normal relations between the sexes." One only has to reflect glancingly on the monstrousness of the relations between the sexes, recorded in a torrent of studies, to absorb the impact of that usage of "normal."

There is, then, a sequence of progressively ideologized pairs pertaining to sexual characteristics and/or behaviours. An incomplete set might include: a hypothetical *x/y* to "neutrally" describe chromosomal differences, *male/female, man/woman, masculine/feminine, homosexual/heterosexual*, and so on – wherein we can see, for instance, that a "real man" is something other than that which is merely biologically "male." Finally, we come to the most recent binary pair: *gay/straight*.

When does "gay" come in? George recalls that "gay" as an adjective was in common usage in the 1950s, as in "gay bar," but can't remember it being used as a noun. Yet in Jack Spicer's 1955 poem "An Answer To A Jew":

When asked if I am of the Jew or Goyim,
When asked if I am an enemy of your people,
I would reply that I am of a somewhat older people:
The Gay, who are neither Jew nor Goyim,
Who were cut down in your Lord God Jehovah's first pogrom
Out at Sodom ...

BUT ISN'T it impossible to imagine a world without "homosexuals" and "heterosexuals"? When I was growing up in the 1950s, my Aunt Pearl was the only "divorcée" in the family. The air of sinfulness implied by that word percolated through a hundred familial gatherings. Now for the most part abandoned – both the word and the significance of the phenomenon – the phantasmagoric character of such categories is apparent. Even earlier: "witch," "heretic," "lunatic."

INDEED, I imagine all sorts of plausible alternatives. For example, whatever happened to that scale proposed by Kinsey in the early 1950s? He suggested putting homosexuality, and heterosexuality as well, on a seven-point scale of 0-6.

Imagine, in the absence of "homosexual," the de-

ideologizing effect of casually proclaiming, "I'm about a 2.5."
And the other, without lifting an eyebrow, murmuring, "I think
I'm a 5," as he sets down his hammer and heads for lunch.

I SEEK OUT other more appropriate pairs. Having invented, out
of necessity, exactly such terms, I was predictably delighted by
this passage in Mishima's *Confessions of a Mask*: " . . . two categories: *androphiles*, who are attracted only by adults; and
ephebophiles, who are fond of youths . . . "

THERE ARE deeper ambiguities. Gender itself comes into question. I remember once, at Buddy's, being struck by the respective androgynies of Michael and Jean.
    The latter was a gargantuan middle aged creature who had
pointedly adopted a name which, in its oral form, was indeter-
minate as to gender. Jean's speciality at the pool table was
being able to shoot one-handed, and he/she seemed to take
special delight in easily defeating various cocky young studs
who fancied themselves pool sharks. One evening I recall seeing – well, let's say – *her* in full splendor. She wore a purple T-
shirt that somehow provided a decolletage that made visible the
beginning of her pendulous teats (simply the sagging breasts of
a heavy-set older man). This was complemented by mauve pre-
creased slacks, a petite gold wristwatch strap cutting into her
chubby wrist, heart-shaped glassframes, and a blond perm. In
terms of gender, Jean was like a blur between film frames –
standing back from the table between shots, in pensive repose,
there was an almost grandmotherly air about her; suddenly she
whipped the cue up in one paw, barely sighting the shot, and
pocketed a striped ball, a tough old bird.
    The complement was provided by Michael, who I knew
primarily as a beautiful, long-haired boy. Having dinner
together one night, he described to me how he sometimes
worked the streets as a girl. As he spoke, I could gradually see
his metamorphosis, imagine the silky sheath of a red dress he
might wear, hairdo, earrings, pantyhose. In fact, I recalled hav-

ing visited him a couple of days earlier, and when he opened the doorway – it was dark inside – he was standing there, slender, with tanned limbs, wearing only satiny red bikini underwear, and just behind him in the gloom was a girl, about his age, also in underwear, and similar in shape to him, as though they were brother and sister (*or* sisters, *or* brothers – the apparition continued to shift). The obscenely exciting detail of this drag masquerade on the streets was that when the men who picked "her" up got to the room what they immediately wanted to do was suck his cock. What shall we call *that* sexual preference? Montaigne says, " . . . our beauty, though it demands somewhat different features, is at its best when, boyish and beardless, it can be confused with theirs."

These instants of protean revelation show what a fuss we make, not merely over *homosexual/heterosexual*, but *male/female* itself.

IT WAS upon being asked, "How's your sex life?", and finding himself shocked by the intrusiveness and absurdity of that careless query that George realized that "sex" itself was but an ideological fabrication. Would someone ask, George wondered, "How's your *conversation life*?"

George points out that bedraggled, middle aged housewives in the Bay or Safeway are confronted by magazines (such as *Cosmopolitan* or *Chatelaine*) that demand, "Is Your Sex Life As Good As It Could Be?", forcing them to acquiesce to the assumption that one ought to *have* a *sex life*.

George: "I want to free as much human contact as possible from 'sex' because that category is so ideologized. I'd like a boy to be able to love another boy without being [called] a 'homosexual.' And to love him physically without it being called 'sex.'"

In a motel restaurant, midway between Vancouver and San Francisco – we're in the midst of one of our seasonal migrations down the coast – George elucidates "the central claims of sex-as-ideology: 1) it's essential to your own being and to being 'normal' to have a 'sex life'; 2) it's the deepest possible communication with an other; sex in the culture is thought to be the only deep way of contacting another human being, the only circumstance in which all that has ever been withheld suddenly becomes available; and 3) it embodies the contradiction to drive you crazy: sex is wrong and forbidden."

In passing, George remarks that his childhood desire to touch or "feel up" the other was a bid for power, control. What was I seeking when I longed to touch my adolescent age-mate M., or later, J.-J.? Eros. Aesthetic attraction. How about beauty? No innocent caress in awe? When I think of myself and B., or Pat, or even, with his redoubtable organ, Spencer, whom I praised without prevarication, eliciting from him a shy, pleased smile, I note that the orgasmic ceremonies provided – at least on occasion – *intimacies unique* – in short, "communication," yielding knowledge, as in the biblical locution, "then I knew him."

But that night, perhaps in a dream, George is insisting on the virtues of chaste courtship, medieval vows of vassalage as a model of love. This time he goes too far, succumbing to the temptation to preserve the mystery of love at the expense of the vulgarity of sex. I wake irrationally furious with George, as though we'd actually been arguing all night. In a moment it gives way to the California blue sky, morning coffee, more talk.

OUTSIDE the window of my room in the Cave Springs Motel, I'm presented with today's edition of the-most-beautiful-boy-in-the-world, a blond youth, stripped to the waist, and digging a hole for a hot tub. Given George's perorations against "sex," I almost feel a twinge of guilt about my desire, imagining my friend's ascent to disinterest. But ten days later, on the way back to the motel after a sumptuous repast at the local restaurant, George asks, in a rare moment of mild inebriation, "Where's that boy who was digging the pool last week?"

"Oh, so you noticed?" I'm pleasantly surprised.

"Of course . . . he was beautiful," George explains, a bit woozily.

III
Darkness

Kings of Hell

OF DUANE HARMON, my friend Sidney recalled, "He was the first *dangerous* man I loved." I was just thinking of Duane when Sidney happened to phone.

Scrambling through an old notebook from last summer, when Pat and I were at the seashore, I find that I recorded a conversation in which Pat remembered that Duane's citizen band (CB) radio "moniker" was Blue Baron. I asked my blond friend if he'd ever slept with him. Just once. Did you let him fuck you? I asked. No, I just gave him a blow job, said Pat. In a later edition of this memory, Pat denied having had sex with Duane at all.

But what stayed in Pat's mind more sharply than sex was an incident at the pool table in a bar one night. Duane was annoyed by a spectator who was horsing around, apparently distracting him from the game. So he simply walked up to this unfortunate, but perhaps obnoxious, bystander and decked him with a single blow. Then, without so much as a pause, Duane coolly turned to the green felt surface and made his shot. Pat recounted this little episode with evident awe.

Once, when I was driving Michael to the bus station the morning after he had spent the night at Duane's, I tried to obtain from him an account of being fucked by Duane. Since Michael, an androgynous slim beauty with deep-set gray eyes, knew how to do more with his asshole once he had your cock implanted in him than anyone I'd ever met, who better to ask? Alas, his prose was not equal to the poetry of his posterior, and we could do little more than establish that Duane had indeed screwed him.

I approach a ghost, but first pause in the presence of these "cameo appearances": Sidney, Pat, Michael; I could even add Greg, who, the first time we drove home together, told me that

Duane had picked him up five years earlier when he was fourteen and, as we passed it, pointed out the three-storey stucco beachfront apartment complex in my neighbourhood where Duane briefly inhabited a basement suite.

Digressive storyteller that I am, these momentary guests tempt me with tales of their own. So, for example, just as I'm about to write something about Duane, at that moment Sidney calls to remind me of the date of a meeting or a deadline for an article for the local gay paper. I mention that I'm thinking about Duane. Sidney remembers him. When it comes time to write about Duane, I include Sidney's remark. But isn't it somewhat unfair to simply mention Sidney in passing? After all, I know a good many interesting things about Sidney: seeker after God, veteran political activist, patron of beauty – although he's scrupulously self-critical here as elsewhere, interrupting our conversation in Numbers to cruise a boy at the pool table with the remark, "Excuse me, I'm objectifying someone." He was even, briefly, a convicted embezzler, though this too must be qualified; since his indiscretion occurred at a fiscally sloppy government agency where he was employed and his gains were lavished on dinners for his friends and courting young men, it was impossible to regard this as anything more serious than folly.

If I name Sidney, even though he's only briefly present, won't somebody inevitably ask, "Who's Sidney?" Won't I then be required to digress further, as I've just done? At first, I thought to simply assign the letters "X," "Y" and "Z" to these appearances. After all, such cameos act simply as functions, and anyway I often fall for the romantic device of assigning a letter of the alphabet to represent a beloved. I've always been entranced by texts that protect the identity of their characters by means of an initial. The person so designated is rendered more seductive. Yet, at the same time, he also becomes more abstract, as though he were a geometric figure. But the "X" on one page, who might be Sidney, is not the same person as the "X" on another page, who turns out to be my cruising crony,

Mr. Stevens. As elsewhere in life, identifications are often imprecise, presences frequently haphazard. Perhaps such cameo appearances are best regarded as promises of future narratives.

IF ONE MEASURE of a person's presence among us is his power after death to produce a reverie in those across whom his shadow falls, then Duane was slightly larger than life. But the demonstration of such a proposition will have to be roundabout, for I knew this idol best by the reflection of his glory in those who worshipped him.

I suppose the best place to start, then, is with R., the most splendid of Duane's boys. Actually, I can recall seeing the two of them together only a few times, at Buddy's, strutting through the upstairs crowd, Duane in the lead by a half-step, still fiercely, arrogantly handsome in his early thirties, black leather jacket, a cigarillo clamped between his teeth, greeting his chums with casual noblesse oblige. He had resolutely maintained the shape and gestures he had acquired as a boy, so that, viewed from a distance, he appeared not much different than he must have looked at sixteen or seventeen. R., not yet twenty, was at his shoulder, proudly smirking, learning the gestures of his role model, as they strode among us. "The Eternal passed by in the form of a pimp. The prattle stopped. There was in his supple bearing the weighty magnificence of a barbarian . . . The torso on his hips was a king on a throne . . . " (Genet). But for the bourgeois world, Duane was the monster of a sexual demonology: molester, pimp, rapist.

I HAD OBSERVED R. previously, at a distance, and was struck by his beauty, particularly his hawkish nose which, for some reason, made me register him as "Italianate, c. late sixteenth C. Venetian," as though I were cataloguing a painting. But when I actually met him for the first time, in the Ambassador one summer afternoon, it was a bit of word-play that struck my fancy.

R. had mentioned that he'd ridden here on his bike, which

he'd left chained to the telephone pole outside the bar. In the repertoire of such routines, in which all the utterances are intentionally open-ended – for the purpose of providing "openings," of course – someone at the table, most likely Mr. Stevens, eventually came around to, "So, what're you doing these days?" To which R. promptly replied, "Pedalling my ass."

This ribald pun on "peddling," a subject which, indeed, is what we were asking about, immediately won me over. The innocuous reference to his ass demanded that we imagine that spectacular portion of his anatomy – in fact, as we soon learned, R. was unblushingly known throughout the community as "Wonderbuns," such was his perfection. At the same time, I was touched by the self-deprecation of the cyclist's declaration. Thus we began.

In the course of my visits to R.'s bedroom I gradually learned about his lover, Duane. Naturally, since he was something of a legend in this demimonde, I had not only heard of him by reputation, but had met him on several occasions over the years. Despite the fearsome stories that circulated about him, Duane was, in fact, the epitome of charm. No doubt, in his vast dealings – as a hustler, kept lover, and later a procurer – he had developed a certain delicacy of manner. Indeed, I had availed myself of his services on occasion. He'd stopped at my table, on his way to or from the john perhaps, and I'd offered him a beer – it seemed natural to lay tribute before him – and expressed some interest in a youth I'd seen him sitting with a minute earlier. "Ya wanna meet him?" Duane asked, as though it were simply a matter of casual largesse on his part.

Officially, Duane was among the despised. That is, there were in the press lurid accounts of his crimes. He had a wife, and together, it was alleged, they preyed on teenage boys and young women, loading them up on drugs, and eventually turning them out on the streets. The possible combinations produced by their seductions were left to the reader's imagination. Duane was currently serving a term in Matsqui prison for "living off the avails . . ." R. vehemently denied most of this. He described his own initial meetings with Duane as almost chaste, and far from coercive. It was impossible for me to sleep with R. . without experiencing the vicarious delight of desiring the same smooth flesh as had given pleasure to the fabled Duane.

One night, R. showed me a letter he had just received from Duane in Matsqui. It was written in pencil, on prison stationery, in a semi-illiterate style that affected macho camaraderie. "Hey, Asshole, howya doin?" it began. I'm an absurdly passionate fan of such prose. When, for example, Pat leaves me a note that says, "I was here but now am gone/left my name to turn you on," followed by the postscript, "I really need to talk to you," I treasure it. Even as I was reading the pedestrian details of Duane's incarceration, I had a stab of regret knowing the fate of this letter – in a day or two it would be thoughtlessly crumpled up and tossed into the garbage – and wanted to ask R. to let me be its archivist. It was as if I had a premonition of how few tangible scraps Duane would leave us.

R. imitated not only Duane's gestures, particularly his swaggering walk, but the very structure of his mentor's desire. He had acquired a female companion – a woman several years older than him, who frequented gay bars and had a thirst for male hustlers. As well, R. maintained a clientele of middle aged men, shot smack with increasing frequency, brawled, and cultivated a taste for boys a few years younger than himself.

What awed me about Duane and R.'s love affair was that for both of them homosexuality must have been an unarticulated subject. It was inconceivable that they could permit it to appear in discourse and thus implicitly identify themselves as its votaries. Both of them would almost surely have preferred anything to the possibility of seeing themselves as a couple of faggots – and in fact they had devised a mix of hetero/ephebic desire sheathed in aggressive masculinity. Their passion seemed to me to attain the splendour of a *necessity*. Since neither would choose it willingly, it must have chosen them. The corollary of this theorem is the intimation that homosexuality itself is a necessity.

AROUND the edges of my relationship with R. – having a drink together in Buddy's, toking up in his living room, chatting idly after sex – over the months I accumulated further scraps of Duane's saga.

He had been paroled from jail. Once again he was seen in the bars. He and R. had gone their separate ways. As always, the accounts of his adventures placed him on the edge of death. Duane was in a life-defying car crash. The vehicle had attempted a rail crossing at high speed, driver and passengers no doubt stoned. It was all too easy to imagine. The train had left car and riders mangled, tenuously alive. Hospitals, brain damage, slow and lengthy rehabilitation, rumours that Duane had been returned to our environs as a shadow of his swaggering self.

When I saw him again, I searched his features as people had done with the actor Monty Clift, who, after a similar disfiguring near-fatal crash, had appeared in *The Misfits*, his famous and beautiful face patched together by a plastic surgeon, the lineaments more or less restored, but its ability to yield emotion oddly disjointed. Duane's survival contributed to the myth of immortality that always attaches to those suspected of being demi-gods.

MONTHS go by. Spring again. R. arrives upstairs in Buddy's, looks around, finally notices me and saunters over with that distinctive strut. As is the nature of such alliances, we had drifted apart. Though he is still beautiful, the heroin is beginning to show. His cheeks are hollow, his nose more hatchet-like.

"Oh, you again," he jibes. I reply in kind: "So you're still hanging around here, eh?" The whole farcical fiction turns on the mutual accusation of: you're the kind of person who doesn't have anything better to do than hang around places like this. "I'm not hanging around here," he answers, mock-heatedly. "I'm just seeing who *is* hanging around here." Meaning, namely, me.

In the midst of this ancient ritual of affectionate insult, he pauses long enough to get me to look out the window to admire

his newly acquired car, a beautiful old forest-green Mustang –
again, a taste acquired from Duane – parked next to the windbreak of cottonwoods that lines one side of Buddy's.

ONE DAY, not long after, as I'm absent-mindedly listening to the
radio, the news reports the discovery of a dead man stuffed into
the trunk of his car, nude, beaten to death, and abandoned in
Stanley Park. It's only the next day, scanning the papers, that I
learned of the death of Duane.

BUT IT WAS more than a year later, at the trial of his youthful
murderer, a boy named Nick, when the appropriately sordid
details were dangled before us. The newspapers gloated as
though a king of hell had been slain. The prose was deliciously
pulpy; but then, even conversations about Duane invariably
took on the syntax of the detective magazines I'd read as a boy.
Describing Duane violently silencing someone who had smart-
ed off, Pat reflects, "Yeah, he dummied him"; Duane appears
on innumerable sets "packing a piece"; to a gay-baiting
straight in a bar, Duane reportedly snarls, "Well I'm a fucking
fag, whaddaya fucking want to do about it?" before punching
the guy's lights out.

Most of the proceedings were devoted to blackening Duane's
name in an effort to suggest that he'd come to a deserved end;
indeed, as the press account conceded, "the slaying victim was
as much on trial as the accused." Duane's convictions for "living off the avails of prostitution and keeping a common bawdy
house" were entered into the record; the reporter's declaration
that he "preferred young males for sex and frequently used violence" was allegedly supported by acquaintances of Duane's
who took the stand to say that they saw him strike his "live-in
lover" earlier in the day of his encounter with his slayer; an accountant was produced to testify that his late boss, the owner
of a chain of picture framing shops, had paid Duane extravagant monthly fees "for procuring boys for [the man's] sexual
habits." Thus was the bourgeois readership at once both sanc-

tified in its own mores and titillated by the steamy tidbits of sin from a nearby Atlantis-like underworld – like walking along English Bay in the morning and spotting used condoms amid the seaweed and shards of pottery.

Duane's killer, Nick, was 22 at the time. Clearing away the cluttered preoccupation with Duane's lack of respectability, it was possible to piece together the events on the night of his murder. Nick had met him at Numbers. On the stand, according to the press, Nick "said he had not 'formally' met Duane before that night, but knew him to see him and was familiar with his reputation, which was the subject of previous testimony ... Despite that, [Nick] said he was only 'leery' of Duane and found him quite friendly during the hours they spent together." Attentive reader that I am, I thought: how perfect those uses of "formally" and "leery," how homey that "knew him to see him."

Nick said Duane had gone home with him – to a bachelor suite in one of the nearby apartment towers – "to drink rye and share some cocaine he had purchased." Nick's roommate Ronnie was already there when they arrived, drunkenly asleep just a few feet away. The friendliness "ended when Duane made overt advances to him in his apartment and he had to fight him off."

Although the prosecutor had produced a witness who said Nick "told him he led Duane to believe he would exchange sexual favors for cocaine," Nick told the jury "he was heterosexual and would not prostitute himself to support his cocaine habit." This produced sneering guffaws on the street where it was common knowledge that Nick hustled. But the motive remained murky.

It was obvious that the deal was cocaine for a fuck, but did Nick plan to rip him off – unlikely, given Duane's handiness with his fists – or did he just go coke crazy, or was it something else altogether? I discounted the bar theories that it might have been an arranged hit; the scene was too haphazard. The fact that Duane was naked, argued the prosecutor, supported the "theory that [Nick] had agreed to some sexual act in return for cocaine, but had then changed his mind and resisted." More likely, although such crucial details were too delicate to be openly speculated upon in a "family" newspaper, there had been some sex already, maybe a b.j. I found some justice in the thought that the killer had at least sucked the cock of his victim, even while his roommate slept. Then Nick had panicked when it became clear Duane was going to fuck him.

In any case, Nick "said he reached for a sawed-off baseball bat and hit Duane on the head, stunning him." At this point, the account of the murder becomes ambiguous, but the details here are less relevant. Nick claimed he woke up his roommate, Ronnie, who finished Duane off. There was the predictable conflicting testimony about who did what. As the prosecutor put it with a rhetorical flourish, it was a "classic" situation of "two men in a room with a dead body and each is pointing the finger at the other." Irrespective, the pathologist testified that Duane had been hit across the head twenty times, and that all but the first one or two blows had been delivered after he lost consciousness because "it was obvious from the parallel pattern that the head was not moving when struck."

After that brutal moment, the tale turns almost lyrical. Nick then left his roommate with Duane's body and "ran nine blocks to another apartment to discuss what had happened with his friend [Scott]." He went back to his own place where he and his roommate carried the nude corpse downstairs and dumped it in the trunk of Duane's car, which Nick drove first to his friend Scott's, then into Stanley Park where he abandoned it at Lost Lagoon. After that, Nick left an easily pursued trail across the border toward his parents in California.

One final vignette, buried in the newspaper prose, caught my eye.

"During the stop at Scott's, Nick said he opened the trunk and took a silver chain and cross from around Duane's neck."

Said Nick: "I saw the crucifix gleaming at me and I didn't think a person that evil should have something like that, so I took it off and gave it to Scott."

Gleaming? Yes, we knew Duane as a creature of mirrors. Johns thought him charming, enemies feared him, lovers were thrilled by the air of danger he exuded, hustlers who emulated his style saw in Duane a model of courage, fags occasionally saw him as their protector.

The jury found Nick guilty of manslaughter. He was sentenced to four years.

AT NIGHT, in some bar (a new one that opened last week), while casually cruising, I run into an old crony who knew Duane and we reminisce, evoking that emissary from the dark side of Eros. It's the world turned upside down, where evil is not quite "evil" as understood in the realm of respectable reason. Buddy's, Celebrities, Numbers: names ranging from intimacy to fame – a kind of anonymity – to the true obscurity of the nameless. Across these pleasure palaces falls the shadow of Duane.

A LONG CAR pulls away from the curb in a blur; as I'm stepping through the glass doors of an apartment tower, I get a glimpse of R. in the passenger's seat, slightly gaunt from dope, being whisked away, as though to his fate.

Porn

IN ONE OF my favourite porno films, *Young and Ready* (a mid-
seventies production), David and Tom meet on a southern California beach. Both in their late teens, David is a blond with a
Disneyland T-shirt and cut-offs; Tom is barechested, tattooed
(a black panther head on his left bicep), and has dark hair. His
faded cut-off jeans sport an enticing tear across the cheek of his
right buttock. After a moment of serious and friendly
conversation, the two make their way up a set of cement steps
toward a cluster of beach condos.

Once inside the oceanfront apartment, there is a moment of
playful, but awkward nuzzling (they seem shy about kissing)
before Tom slips behind the bar and begins mixing drinks
while David perches on a captain's stool. How the two of them
have landed in these affluent middle class surroundings is never
indicated, but the pornmaker can probably safely assume that
sociological consistency is not a major viewer demand.

Tom emerges from behind the counter and – as the gooey
advertising copy in the brochure promoting this film asks,
"What happens when two young guys reach the age when their
sexual appetites become insatiable?" – David gropes Tom's
crotch, and a moment later as Tom's cut-offs slide to the floor,
giving way to white briefs, which are also pulled off, his oblig-
ingly hard cock becomes available. After David, in various pos-
tures, blows Tom, positions are reversed. With David stretched
out on the shag carpet, Tom skilfully and vigorously goes down
on him.

In the next set of scenes, we're in the bedroom. "Tom is still
super horny and wants to show David the fun of anal sex,"
claims the copy writer. David is at first lying on his side, while
Tom, who through a bit of minor bedroom gymnastics is
behind and at a tangent to him, has his cock deeply implanted

in David's ass. In the genital close-ups, we are offered the textural contrast of David's smooth white ass, bordered by tanline at the waist, against Tom's pulsating furry inner thigh muscle, then zoom to Tom's hard cock, with its thick inflated undervein, gently but relentlessly entering David's hole, followed by slow withdrawal of the camera eye to David's golden thigh looped over Tom's coltishly bony knee to give him easier access to David's butt.

As they shift from one position to another – both on their sides but now facing each other, David's feet on Tom's shoulders – there is an occasional bit of amiable banter between them that seems to indicate that there is nothing coercive about the situation, nor, as is proven by some outright mutual giggling, are they "distanced," as sometimes happens during sex. That is, the scene appears to say, "I have my cock in you"/ "I know you have your cock in me." At one point, Tom is on his knees, erect cock still in David's ass, and David is on his belly sprawled half off the bed, humping his butt up into Tom's crotch.

During the long climactic scene, David is on his back with his legs in the air, knees drawn up to his chest, ankles resting on Tom's shoulders, caressing the arms of the boy fucking him, while Tom, deep inside David, simply arches his back, thus lifting his own ass, and then dropping it, to deep-hump David. From one camera angle directly behind Tom, before the eye closes in under Tom's ass to show his cock repeatedly entering his partner's hole, one sees the slightly soiled soles of David's feet just above Tom's shoulders.

"As Tom plows David's virgin ass," says the copy, "they both get hotter than they have ever been before." Although one is never as much of an expert in these matters as one would like (or claim) to be, it's doubtful that David's ass is as virgin as the film's sponsors allege. As for the degree of heat attained, Tom seems properly enthusiastic, and after a series of vigorous final thrusts, he pulls his cock from David's ass at the last minute and comes over his butt. Shortly afterwards, David jacks himself off while Tom lays alongside him, pinning David's thigh between his knees, and caressing the boy's balls.

There's a last jerky cut to the shower stall where Tom and David are soaping each other. Tom carefully and creamily massages David's firm well-shaped bum, while David washes Tom's chest. There is considerable exuberant horsing around as Tom wiggles up against David's butt in a playful parody of their recent fucking. A few feet of California beach at sunset concludes this erotic epic.

ADMITTEDLY, my bucolic description of *Young and Ready* is a far cry from the polemic set out in recent and critical accounts of pornography. This is not to deny that gay porn shares with all porn many of its politically deplorable elements. Like porn-in-general, it too is obsessive: its compulsive focus is on sex; idealistic: only the near perfect are offered to public view; and economically exploitative of the performers.

But what demarcates, and perhaps absolves, gay male porn from the rest are the following features:

a. It doesn't degrade women. While, at first, that seems but a tautology, does it not, in fact, answer the fundamental feminist objection of the campaign against pornography?

b. It shows male homosexuality. Again, merely an apparent truism but, despite all, the presence of gay porn defies the prohibition against the appearance of homosexual sex, which is also a prohibition against its existence, thus disturbing the existing social order of heterosexual supremacy.

c. It is more democratic. That is, I'm repeatedly struck by the fact that gay porn offers a portrayal of sex that is often more reciprocal, less predictable, less role-enforcing than its counterparts. For example, in *Young and Ready*, David and Tom mutually suck each other's cocks; if, according to some code of "manhood," cocksucking is a humiliation, homosexuality apparently refuses to acknowledge the roles that might be upheld by this taboo. Again and again, we are presented with such reversals and mutualities. Even where positions are maintained (fucker/fucked), there is often an expression of affection that unsettles rigid boundaries. Entering the fray, my banner bears the inscription: *Equalities, reciprocities, reversals.*

d. So, also, are the viewer's possible identifications made pluralistic here. If, in heterosexual porn, the male viewer is constrained to inhabit the image of the fucker and never that of the penetrated, in gay porn one identifies with any and all present, sometimes shifting perspective in mid-scene, or joining Tom and David as a third.

OSTENSIBLY, we have a drama: two boys meet each other on the beach, agree to have sex, go to a beach apartment, etc. Although in this "period" of porn – its "primitive" phase, prior to its integration into the mode of capitalist mass distribution – the dramatization is quite shabby; nonetheless, however crudely, these events are "scripted." In "real" life, they didn't meet on the beach, etc. Though the sex is scripted too, it is more. It is, in a sense, a documentary of their sex. Their "real" lives as pornographic actors coincide with the "characters" they've been hired to play. I find myself looking for moments not required by the "script" – bits where some unplanned playful teasing occurs, as, for example, the horseplay in the shower between David and Tom, which seems tacked on, a sort of "home movie" afterthought that functions as a sign of their non-scripted relationship. Such "uncalled for" exchanges tend to stand out (especially since the young actors are clearly amateurs) and seemingly serve to "soften" the brutality of the commercial arrangement. This may only be, I recognize, a sentimental interpretation on my part.

The doyen of gay porn reviewers, who signs himself Mingus, confirms my thought that "pornography is *essentially* a branch of documentary filmmaking." It would be technically possible to have mock-porn through special effects, fake cum, etc., but Mingus agrees that "simulated sex would probably not work in a porn film," to say nothing of how unnecessarily cumbersome it would be to arrange when the real is so easily at hand.

"Somehow the essence of a porn film is that it is documenting a real sexual event," Mingus observes, and adds, "which in an odd way means that at least some gay pornography is precisely the opposite of fantasy."

If I notice their "real" lives poking through the scripted fantasy, then I must also imagine those lives beyond the documented instant. David and Tom, if alive, are now about 30. Where are they? Have they been struck by the plague? What are they doing?

WATCHING *Young and Ready* or similar productions, I'm entranced by the minimalist plots and simple-minded, often non-synch dialogue in these films. My mentor, Mingus, on the other hand, suffers through the "acting" with "the numbing sense of sitting through a junior high school production of Shakespeare, and a bad one at that." I find myself mentally rewriting the dialogues to make them sexier, more complex, nakedly confessional.

ONE MORNING I was meditating on a still porn photo from *Young and Ready* that fascinated me. Tom is standing on the bed while David is on his knees, ass raised, torso slanted forward, resting on his right elbow and forearm, head of tousled blond hair turned as if to get a peek at Tom who is just about to enter his asshole. Tom's left leg is bent and striding forward, the right one is tautly held back for balance, while his right hand at the base of his cock guides it towards David's hole, and his left one rests lightly on David's bent back. In a second, in order to achieve the proper angle from which to stick his dick into David, Tom will have to drop to his left knee. Meanwhile, if you look closely into David's crotch you can see not just his genital but his hand jacking himself off to make it easier to take Tom's cock.

That evening, my young friend Michael, of his own volition, assumed the identical posture I'd seen in the still, thus bringing the photo delightfully "to life." Yet Barthes declares, "Nothing more homogeneous than a pornographic photograph ... no secondary, untimely object ever manages to half conceal, delay, or distract" the presentation of the one thing, sex, which completely constitutes it. Barthes, however, offers the qualification: "I am not saying the erotic photograph: the erotic is a pornographic that has been disturbed, fissured." In fact, I find few such homogeneous instances; invariably the pornographic photo presents something or someone – most often, simply *the person* – who indeed half conceals, delays, distracts, disturbs. Did not Cafavy find this to be so?

> *In this obscene photograph that was sold*
> *clandestinely on the street (so the police would not see),*
> *how was such a dream of a face found*
> *in this pornographic photograph;*
> *how did you come to be here?*

Barthes' demarcation of the "disturbed, fissured" from the strictly pornographic reminds me of an idea I've been mulling over. In what I regard as a misguided effort to exonerate certain portions of porn, the erotic has been given, so to speak, a bad name. I mean, the current tendency to delineate the erotic as a sort of "good porn" – not demeaning, not oppressive, wholesome – seems to me mistaken. That is, porn is porn, both the objectionable and the wholesome versions. If there are distinctions to be made, let them be in terms of "good," "bad," "hot," "demeaning," or whatever critical vocabulary develops, rather than defining porn as a tautology of the disapproved. What identifies porn is its singular, or even compulsive, attention to sexual representation, separated from the rest of social reality. What is the erotic then? Those representations – the films *Sunday, Bloody Sunday* and *My Beautiful Laundrette* are instances displaying the homoerotic – which integrate sexuality into a social totality.

I ESPECIALLY like looking at the photographs of the beloveds of writers. Here is a snapshot of a young man in a white bathing suit, the material bunched in the crack of his ass, his back to us, standing at a railing overlooking the water somewhere in Italy in the 1930s, the lover of one of the English poets of the day. Here's a trick of Tennessee Williams', a companion of Whitman's, or T. at Fisherman's Wharf in San Francisco a quarter century ago. The enchantment of this meta-literary activity perhaps comes from the optical illusion that one is gazing upon a photograph of the Muse.

An odd corollary: someone I once knew gives me some old photos from when we worked in a warehouse long ago. Both of those in which I appear are so badly focused as to be almost unrecognizable. In one I'm in a flannelette shirt and khaki dungarees, opening my lunch bag while standing in front of a park bench; in the other I'm holding a cigarette and the sleeve of my polo shirt is rolled up to show a muscular bicep. I can almost see my beauty, which I was unaware of at the time, and at the same time, before the unfocused quality of the photos allows me to identify myself, I simply see a handsome young man for whom, *now*, before I slowly discern it is myself, I feel a flash of lust, as though for anyone I might be attracted by. How exciting – almost a form of incest – to desire one's *past self*.

Whether as a trace of a desire or something else, the essence of the photo, observes Barthes, was a "scientific discovery [that silver halogens were sensitive to light] that made it possible to recover and print directly the luminous rays emitted by a variously lighted object . . ."; thus "the photograph is literally an emanation of the referent . . . [i.e.], from a real body, which was there, proceed radiations which ultimately touch me." If the photo is a clarity, a proof of what-has-been, then the memory of desire is a fuzziness, a half-light, a did-it-happen?

BETTER YET: strippers, hustlers on streetcorners, first-night stands. In observing the erotic function of the theatre, Barthes notes that it "alone of all the figurative arts presents the bodies and not their representations . . . you would merely need to be momentarily crazy in order to jump onto the stage and touch

119

what you desire." Whereas, cinema is "like those bodies which pass by, in summer, with shirts unbuttoned to the waist: *Look but don't touch.*"

BUTCH blond Pat, his hard-on in a rubber – a precaution seldom observed on the sets of the imagination – kneeled behind Fraser, who was on his hands and knees in bed, his long cock growing stiff in my hand as Pat vigorously humped him – most of which resembled the world portrayed in the videos. Having noted that the "acting" in porn is "simply dreadful," Mingus observes that "all this changes when the boys drop their pants and get into sex, and in this porn imitates life."

But, as well, life imitates porn. Long before Pat inaugurates the festivities by unzipping his fly and pulling out his dick, I'd often endure the atrocious scatalogical joking of the two of them, imitation farting included, a caricature of the bedtime talk of very young boys at summer camp, or I'd listen to boring disquisitions on the state of the dope market. Even in bed, on the verge of a transformation into "Ganymedes brimming with passion and play," as Mingus puts it, they had an infuriating ability to maintain the pretence, in the name of preserving their macho social personas, that they weren't at all the sort of persons just about to slurp and suck and lick each other's flesh. As well, real-life porn presents us with continuities beyond the filmic spectacle: living with the "actors" after the cameras and lights are shut off.

Having been raised on *Aesop's Fables*, almost inevitably a maxim suggests itself to encapsulate the meaning of this scene, namely: Porn is a utopia . . . until it arrives in person.

Death

MUCH younger, but after I'd already begun to write, I imagined myself at some future, though not impossibly distant, time, having acquired such a wealth of experience and proficiency in my craft that I would find myself, if not effortlessly, at least with some confidence or naturalness of manner, addressing the "great subjects": Love, Death, Beauty, Truth, God . . .

How I envied the author of "When I Pay Death's Duty," who declared with seeming certainty,

> *It won't be complete darkness because there*
> *isn't any. One thing will stop and that's this*
> *overweening pride in the peacock flesh . . .*

or, in my case, not pride, at least not in *my* flesh, but the ceaseless desire for, and pursuit of, "the peacock flesh" of the other.

> *And when I pay death's duty*
> *the love I never conquered*
> *when young will end as such.* (Blaser)

MOSTLY, though, death appeared to me (then as now) a particularly intractable, ultimately unsolvable, indeed senseless, puzzle in logic. There is no good reason for it. Since my fate is little different from that of my black cat, Dab – who, this very moment, sits sedately on the mock-Persian carpet in the next room – what need do I have, with respect to death, of human consciousness?

I WAS ONCE in bed with a curly-haired blond youth who had recently read Herman Hesse's *Siddhartha*. He asked me how long Buddha had lived. Then in a quizzical afterthought, he inquired if indeed the enlightened one had come to an earthly end. "Yes, everybody dies," I found myself saying. "There's suffering, sickness, old age and death for everyone," I reported, having myself already been the beneficiary of some of these Four Noble Gifts.

WITTGENSTEIN would probably say (or has said – I refuse to go rummaging for the reference) that my "problem" with death is but a problem in language. The task is not to solve, but to *dissolve* the puzzle, he'd insist. Though the inability to make sense of death may indeed be a syntactical dilemma of sorts, there is yet a residue. As my friend Tom observes, "Though we cannot make sense of it, we nonetheless sense it . . . "

WAKING from an afternoon nap, I find myself worrying whether the instant chocolate mousse pie has chilled in the fridge, while simultaneously sneering at my use of packaged mousse. "How tacky; did I really do that?" Then the thought of death comes to me. Or, in the early evening, in the background drone of the first period of the Maple Leafs-Red Wings game on TV, something brushes my sleeve and the thought of death curls like my cigarette smoke. Or, on the screen, I see a man in a hospital, somewhere in the epicentre of the plague, translucent tubes in his nose. Here, at the periphery of the epidemic, I'm engaged in a calculus of probabilities: time over geography multiplied by partners over acts equals degree of risk, only to think, I wouldn't like to have tubes in my nose.

MUCH younger, skipping down the slanting streets, singing, "Death, where is thy sting-a-ling-ling?" (Behan).

The Black Diaries

NOTICING the sparseness of my notebook entries – "Last night,
M. Sex, dinner, movie." – I think of the "Black Diaries" of
Roger Casement.

Perhaps each of us locates one historical figure with whom,
because of various correspondences of character or uses of the
language, he most identifies. Casement, British consul in various outposts – I savour the glamour of Boma, Madeira,
Lourenço Marques on my tongue – was an officer of the state,
political writer, amorous subject, revolutionary.

Entering Conrad's heart of darkness, he travelled the Congo,
1903, meticulous gatherer of the evidence of the atrocities in
the rubber plantations of Leopold's African kingdom. Back in
London, he feverishly penned the *Congo Report*, 6,000 words at
a sitting. In between, he cruised for boys in the parks.

He attended to the chopped off stubs of the forearms of
rubber workers with the same gravity that he caressed the
weighty members of the youths he met in the dark gardens and
lanes of the port cities where he had served. Not the work of
madmen, or the aberrantly cruel, he reported, but an expression of a *system* of horror.

Later, Casement performed a similar inquiry along Peru's
Putumayo. Occasionally he wrote verse, not appreciably better,
but probably no worse than that of other cultured gentlemen
of his era. An Irish nationalist, he was eventually hung for his
part in the uprising of 1916. Sentence would have been com-
muted, but the "Black Diaries," shown to George V, the Arch-
bishop of Canterbury and other suitably shocked worthies,
squelched efforts on his behalf. Thus, we have this use to which
language is put:

> Turned in together at 10.30-11 – after watching bil-
> liards. Not a word said till – "wait I'll untie it" and then

"Grand". Told many tales and pulled it off on top grand-
ly.

   Rode gloriously, splendid steed. Huge, told of many.
"Grand".

   . . . huge and curved and he awfully keen. X 4/6'

   Millar, again. First time he turned his back. "Grand"
back, voluntarily.

   July 28. Hotel. Splendid testiminhos. *Soft as silk and*
big and full. No bush to speak of. Good wine needs no
bush.

   . . . then Senate Square and Caboclo (boy 16-17) seized
hard. Young, stiff, thin.

   Dinner at 8 p.m. and out to cemetery and met Friend
who entered at once. Huge testiminhos. *Police passing*
behind paling – but he laughed and went deeper. $10.

Each spare detail enchants me: the use of "paling," the realness
of the nearby cops, the laughter of the boy who fucks him
which echoes down the decades along the paths we have also
cruised. Casement wrote it down, his biographer notes, so that
he could again savour the pleasure when rereading: "He would
sometimes add an exclamation of delight in the margin, later."

Buddy

budd'y, n. (colloq.). (Usu. as familiar
form of address) brother, chum, mate. [dim.
of *bud*, childish pronunc. of *brother*]

A BLACK Americanism, dates back to the mid-nineteenth century, the time of Whitman; although in continuous colloquial
use, "buddy" appears in the *Oxford English Dictionary* only in
the 1950s, probably as a result of widespread usage in World
War II as a term of friendship or simply matehood among sol-
diers; also employed as a proper name, i.e., Buddy; in the
1980s, the definition darkens – principally among gays – to refer to the partner who, often through an agency organized for
such a purpose, commits himself to friendship with a person
with AIDS, as in, "buddies program."

On Friendship

I WAS OFFERED the cheering sight of the poet – my friend George – dancing on his 50th birthday. The tune gave impetus to his jerky, bucking movements, lifting his hands – the wrists loose – simultaneously with a leg, a bent knee, but in any case, moving freely, not protecting his body from injury or ridicule. Was it not as he had once written?

> I danced,
> drunkenly, to your Irish Country,
> a jar of Guinness in my right hand
>
> splashing/I
> fell on my ass, there was
>
> mixed applause. Mixed with forbearance.
>
> "We pretended we didn't know you,"
> you said. Oh, Mike, I
> was pretending
>
> from way back.

He thus appears to me both courageous and resourceful, two qualities we seek in our friends, if not our lovers.

". . . THE IDENTITY of each friend, which made that friend *lovable*, was based upon a delicately proportioned and henceforth absolutely original combination of tiny characteristics organized in fugitive scenes, from day to day. Thus each friend deployed in [my] presence the brilliant staging of his originality" (Barthes).

SITTING next to me in the passenger's seat, as we're making one of our seasonal coastal migrations south on Interstate-5, out of the corner of my eye I watch George reading a book about economics or artificial intelligence, pen in hand to slashingly underline a certain passage, fingertips scratching like a bird at the corner of a page to turn it.

"IT IS RARE good fortune, but inestimably comforting, to have a worthy man of sound understanding and ways that conform with yours, who likes to go with you," says Montaigne, on the pleasure of a travelling companion.

GEORGE, PATRICK and I are walking along First Avenue in Seattle. It's Pat's first time here; I hope he enjoys it. On our way to a perfect bar, George unaffectedly and learnedly discourses on the relation between architectural styles, economics and the history of Seattle. Our magical guide brings it alive, simultaneously creating and opening up the city before our eyes. George glows; Pat, usually uninterested in intellectual analysis, is engrossed. I'm delighted: by the generosity of George's erudition; that Pat visibly appreciates this gift; that Pat – blond, beautiful, twenty – is happy. The streets, rows of shabby buildings a moment ago, are suddenly real.

GEORGE READS to me:

> Well, when I had to explode,
> I would explode,
> and there they would be
>
> my mother's family
> Emmett & Frank & Marie
> alive & dancing
> eating & drinking
>
> I didn't call it a miracle. They were shades
> & thru them I could see the smoking ruins
> & feel the pain/I have never felt.

Poetry, an almost lost pleasure, gives us the sense of being transported, admitted to an innermost sanctum, taken underground, travelling in a time machine – contemporaneous with Homer's Odysseus at the bloody fosse in Hades.

THE USUALLY sage Bud Mordden, author of *I've A Feeling We're Not In Kansas Anymore*, observes about friendship, "Perhaps it's a matter of simple arithmetic; after ten or twelve years, you've already fought about everything potentially available, and can settle back and just get along." Nonetheless:

George and I are having a really bad scene. Perhaps it was my fault. I had delightedly spent the last morning of our trip to San Francisco interviewing a porn actor who was the subject of an article I was writing. Now, driving north, I was brainlessly babbling away, "And you know what the secret of sucking your own cock is? It's not the length of the cock, it's the length and suppleness of the neck," I report. I'm overjoyed by the discovery of this idiotic bit of wisdom; George is seething.

By evening, at a restaurant in Dunsmuir, California, where we had once seen and admired a beautiful blond boy, George, his mind detonated by three martinis, his voice just a shade beneath the decibel-level of yelling, is spitting, "Gay. I hate it, I hate it, I hate it. Porn. I hate it, I hate it, I hate it."

The next day, driving from Dunsmuir to Portland, Oregon, George reports to me that he awoke at two in the morning, his mind "shattered," and then spent the rest of a sleepless night attempting to "reconstruct" it. He's pale with exhaustion. Now, it's I who am furious, oddly enough, about how reserved he is in the expression of his affection for me. "Then, what is this about?" I ask through tight lips, and there is no ambiguity that by "this" I mean our friendship. There's a pause. "Love, I guess," George affirms. I let my breath out.

Nonetheless, he accuses me of devotion to a "cult of the phallus," as opposed to activities – politics, religion – "of general social significance." I'll have to go back to Plato's *Symposium*, the only place in discourse where our attraction to physical beauty is directly connected to love of the beauteous city and, beyond that, to love of the beautiful itself.

MONTAIGNE SAYS of his friend, "If I were pressed to say why I love him, I feel that my only reply could be: Because it was he, because it was I."

ONE DAY, George announces to me that, growing older, he finds himself giving up his illusions.
"Which illusions?" I want to know.
"Well, first, the illusion of immortality."
"What else?"
"The illusion that words mean something." He goes on to slightly modify that statement, but I miss it, thinking of my next question.
"Is love an illusion?"
"No," George immediately replies. A moment later, he adds, "I have a new definition of love." I wait. "Love is the compassionate understanding of the discord between the heart and the world."

MONTAIGNE: "I like the idea of Archytes, that it would be unpleasant to be even in heaven and to wander among those great and divine celestial bodies without the presence of a companion."

How The Plague Ended: A Science Fiction

ONE DAY a politician I knew phoned me and said, "The plague is over, for us."

It was true, in a way.

By "us," he meant gays who so far – by luck, circumstance and the newly crafted old wives' tale called "safe sex" – had avoided exposure to the agent of the sickness.

It wasn't over for those of "us" who were dying or about-to-be-dying. Nor was it over for groups of people the bureaucracy of the plague described as "marginalized," or for vast populations around the world. But for gay males in North America, sometime in the late 1980s the rate of lethal transmission, or more technically, of conversion from "seronegative status" for the alleged marker of the sickness to "seropositive," had dropped to almost nil. New infections had, for all practical purposes, ceased. A public health official announced the removal of gays from the official roster of "risk groups." (How easily we had acquired the vocabulary of the plague; its semi-technical terms rolled off our tongues almost without a second thought, though a few linguists of the resistance challenged its lexicon, explored the political ramifications of acceding even to the image of the "plague.")

It was, if such a word can be used, something of a triumph in the self-education of a community, or perhaps the fact that the "sight of a noose can concentrate the mind wonderfully." Yet even now, nearly a decade after its appearance, it was a still-mysterious affliction. Thus, it hadn't ended with a magic bullet, a cure, or even imperfect treatments. In fact, the search for an imperfect treatment to rescue the dying and about-to-be-dying continued in laboratories everywhere. It ended, so it was said, because we had changed. And the change had changed us, in ways that were not yet apparent.

We didn't even feel relief. Perhaps we permitted ourselves to take note of our exhaustion, especially in the epicentres where the plague had ravaged communities beyond recognition, where the grievers knew they simply couldn't attend one more memorial service, and then went. For some, I suppose, there was faint regret, for the pestilence, oddly enough, had given new meaning to their lives or, to echo Cavafy, was "a kind of solution."

What next? We couldn't yet turn our attention back to the everyday catastrophes of economics, politics, mortality. We would be burying our dead for another five years. We would continue to sit in committees, answer hotlines, display the quilted names of the dead in cities across the land. We would, if need be, draft yet another pamphlet assuring the public that it was not transmitted by "casual contact"; if need be – and no doubt, need would be – we would demonstrate once more for the release of "promising drugs."

We had not ceased desiring during the plague, though we had been baffled by how it was possible to continue desiring in the midst of its horror. My favourite porn reviewer had ceased publishing – there were too many dead in New York for reportage of such recreations to be other than an absurdity. Yet, we would continue to desire. We had not ceased grieving during the war; we would continue to cry our eyes out. We would find ourselves numbly staring at the water on a muggy afternoon, then come to, recalling a dinner engagement. Gradually, it would become a memory, like the curling, yellow-edged pages of an old newspaper exposed to the air. But when it ended, we barely noticed.

Ghost Site

AS HE'S UNDRESSING by the side of the bed, stepping out of his jeans, one leg slightly lifted, his torso bent forward, weight balanced on the other leg, ass bare as the denim peels away, M.'s arms extend, reaching down to slip the pant leg under his foot. I think there's a movement in ballet that resembles this figuration. At the moment, the only word that occurs to me is *plié*. In a second he'll be nude except for white socks, trimmed at the top in stripes of primary colours (red, blue), evocative of the winged feet of naked Hermes and reminiscent, perhaps intentionally so, of younger undressed boys horsing around in the changing room by the swimming pool, their erotic quality enhanced by absence of self-knowledge of their beauty. We each bear in mind a series of such "poses" of the beloveds, like snapshots in a wallet.

In that casual instant, otherwise mostly taken up with anticipation, I notice the slack of M.'s stomach musculature, a ripple of flab (incipient toll of dissolute adventures), and the way the light seeping into the room turns his flesh pale gray. Desire gazes into a ghost site. The moment of assessment quickly gives way to his mastery, care, old knowledge of lovemaking. A less grandiose version: pre-noon dope, beer, sex.

Afterwards, from the next room, where he's getting a cigarette, he calls out, "Am I getting fat?" "Come in here and let me see you," I say, still in bed. He enters, age twenty, awaiting judgment. True, there's additional weight, his legs have grown sturdier, the flesh is looser, but most of all, his shape is changing out of its lambent glory, is, as he says, "filling out." Gone: those graceful limbs, rounded tight butt – fascinating even to himself only a year ago as he revelled in his reflection before a full-length mirror.

Elsewhere too: in Buddy's last night, I'm bored watching

young men in the latest and most ridiculous fashions, even as I find myself accepting the current haircuts. The most recent spurt of redecoration features a "floating island" bar upstairs; more gleaming, cold surfaces, fewer images. I can imagine it going on without me. I can picture myself driving by where it used to be, long after it has ceased to exist, perhaps briefly recalling a night of shimmering beauty, and almost as quickly forgetting it as I head downtown on an errand.

In the lane between Buddy's and Numbers, as I cross over, the night is flecked with wisps of the plague and the air carries a current hit tune whose refrain asks,

> *What's love*
> > *got to do*
> *Got to do*
> > *with it?*

reminding me for the thousandth time that even in this pop form, poetry can tell two or more stories at once, so that while we hear the banal plaint we also discern the image of Love's Labours: what does love have to do?

Inside again, the air smoky; on one screen, porn as decor, on others, perpetual rock videos; not even the stairways, corridors, crannies, zones – a Casbah – serve to distract me from the recognition that these bodies are as abstract as the name of the bar promises they will be (Numbers).

Past midnight, bedded down alone, even Roland Barthes, the author who first inspired these reflections, disappoints me. What appeared so charming earlier, now as frequently seems annoyingly precious. My enthusiasms dissipate: for the amorous discourse, semiotics of the bar, desire itself. Instead, I find myself thinking about hot deserts, Chopin, landscapes without bodies, implacable death.

This has nothing whatsoever to do with whether or not I *want* M. I do; though desire diminishes, appreciation deepens. "Well?" he asks, knowing the worst. Ignoring the obvious – time's ravages and the inevitable disappearance of the ephebe –

yet retaining the truth, I affirm as lightly as possible, "I love you." Not *in love* with him, of course, though I once was, but simply that I love him, for qualities x, y and z, and for himself.

Desire has passed through these rooms, pages, bodies. It is of the nature of this voyage that the very things that brought me this far drop away. I, too, will, in due course, become a ghost site for you.

Epilogue

AS A BOY, I always liked books with epilogues. I was one of those ardent readers who, having become immersed in the lives of the people in the story, dreaded the impending end of the adventure. Once it was over, I knew, they would be gone forever.

Often, I slowed down the pace of my reading, sometimes restricting myself to but a few sentences per sitting, both to savour and to "save" (myself from) the inevitable end. How pleasant it was, then – the passion of the players spent – to turn the page and be rewarded with the bonus of an epilogue, in which they reappeared, released from the tension of the story, to be spoken of flatly in terms of their histories.

The logic of the epilogue also appealed to me. For was it not also so in life that lives went on, beyond the moment of the story that had enchanted us for an evening? Hence, the attraction of epilogues, sequels, series. Could any adolescent who had read Balzac's *Père Goriot* and fallen in love with Eugene de Rastignac, not wonder about his fate as he stood on the heights of Père Lachaise cemetery with all "Paris spread out below on both banks of the winding Seine . . . the evening lights beginning to twinkle here and there"? And what happened to Vautrin, the thief who had engaged Rastignac in amatory conversations in a garden? What good news to learn that if only one went on to read the subsequent *Lost Illusions*, the young man who threw down the gauntlet to society, and the legendary thief who had desired him, would both return.

What hadn't occurred to me when *Buddy's* (or *Eros/Cupid* as I sometimes thought of it) was published in the spring after I finished writing it, was that the epilogue might consist, not of what afterwards befell its heroes, but of the characters' criticisms of the book itself. I had fallen, I must confess, into thinking of *Eros/Cupid* as simply a novel, one bearing the standard disclaimer, "Any resemblance to persons living or dead. . ." The trouble I'd taken to invent a genre that disregarded the conventional boundaries between fiction and fact, narrative and exposition, had completely slipped my mind. Instead, I thought of *Buddy's* as a story made up purely of my imaginings about the narrator's curious love for two young men, Mel and Bret, and his enduring friendship with George, the poet who provided the measure of all affections. I utterly forgot that the figures of that narrative might come back in person to haunt me.

THE FIRST HINT came one Sunday afternoon (I was already working on a new book about local politics) when I saw Sidney at a meeting of a writers' group to which we belonged called Sodomite Invasion. He reported that the night before he had bumped into an enraged minor character from my book, an ex-lover of Mel's, darkly threatening a range of actions from legal to violent. Ron and Tod and Nathaniel, the other writers in the group, were amused and impressed by this bit of gossip, proving, as it did, that life was perfectly prepared to avenge itself on art.

Sure enough, just as I was settling down to work the next day (and starting to worry about deadlines), the phone rang. The man at the other end of the line, Ray, was simultaneously aggrieved that I'd invaded his private life, insulted by my offhand description of his "only redeeming feature" being "a rather terrifying and simultaneously thrilling piledriver/jackhammer style of fucking," and prepared to debate the nature of literature.

"But I didn't use your name or give the address of your store," I lamely began my retreat. "I'm sure there are lots of gay, young businessmen who run frame shops. No one will know."

"My friends will," he grimly replied. And anyway, he had since gone on to a more sensitive posting in government service. Furthermore, what gave me the right to claim that his only virtue was his ability to fuck? "Do you even know me?" he demanded.

Aw-oh, I thought to myself, gritting my teeth as he rattled off the bill of particulars. "Well, no, of course not," I admitted, as another part of my mind drifted off to a sophomoric philosophical consideration along the lines of, what does it mean to know someone? In fact, I'd only seen him once, standing at the back of his store, the time I'd come by to pick up Mel, just long enough to observe and later write that he was a "slim, muscular, mustachioed man in his mid-twenties."

"Well, how could you say that my 'only redeeming feature' – "

"But that's not exactly what I meant," I babbled. Did he have the book open in front of him to the very page as he was conducting this textual exegesis? How do you explain to an angry ex-businessman and ex-fling that one of the semifictional devices of the narrative is the hapless narrator's envy of Mel's lovers? Was he likely to be mollified by a discussion of irony? "I mean, I'm sure you have many, uh, 'redeeming', uh..."

"For example," he cut in, "I'm an environmentalist."

All this for one, measly paragraph? But admittedly, I hadn't imagined viewing any of it from his point of view.

Ray was becoming impatient with my sputtering. "What is the purpose of this book?" he asked with finality.

Good question. I was struck dumb. While mentally debating the options, which seemed to come down to defending truth and beauty or simply confessing that I was a mean-spirited gossip out to destroy lives and reputations, Ray interjected, "Anyway, I don't think gay life should be written about."

The sinking feeling in the pit of my stomach was a premonition that my troubles had only just begun.

MY FRIEND Bob Princeton, a fellow teacher in the philosophy department at the college where I worked, was worried too. He was in his cubbyhole office, heating water in a kettle to make instant noodle soup. "What about the parents?" asked Bob, a rangy, bearded, rabelaisian-tempered best-friend who knew all about nature, machinery, ancient Greece, and free speech law (he assured me that I was unlikely to get sued).

"What *about* the parents?" I asked. "They're not in the book. Anyway, you and Sheila called me from bed the other night to say how much you liked *Buddy's*." Sheila was Bob's wife. "You're parents," I pointed out, as if that clinched the argument.

"The parents of the students," Bob patiently explained. "Besides, Martin's only seven." Martin was Bob's kid. "The parents of the students," he repeated. "What if they get placards and begin picketing the college?"

"You're kidding," I said. He wasn't kidding.

"Okay, what if the press comes up here and asks you, do you sleep with your students? What are you going to say?"

"*Jamais*," I said.

"Never?" he asked, brightening a bit. "What if they ask, have you ever, even once, slept with a student?"

"*Jamais*," I declared.

He nodded approval. "*Jamais*," Bob said, "I like that. That's good. *Jamais*."

I DROVE GREG DOWNTOWN after an afternoon in bed. He was the young man whose form had provided the image used on the cover of *Buddy's*, as well as other pleasures in my life. I parked near the Routledge, a shaggy four-storey hotel just off movie row. The Rut, as it was inevitably called, was the bar where Mel worked, and where I hung out since Buddy's had closed. I'd dropped off a copy of the book for him a few days before. He was wearing a loose white T-shirt and had one of those haircuts all the boys were sporting that spring, shaved along the sides, the top brushed back with gel.

One glimpse was all I needed. Mel had a wounded, glowering look. Even as I dreaded what was to come, I involuntarily noticed that that glowering, wounded look looked pretty good on him.

"Well, how was it?" I asked.

He glanced up, tight-lipped, from behind the bar where he was rinsing beer mugs in a sink. "I didn't like it," he said. Those lush, wet lips were suddenly closed against me.

"But you're the hero," I protested. I might have added, not just the hero, but a god, Cupid himself. Well, okay, a godlet, then, but still. . . In fact, my friend Tod from the writer's group had already poured scorn on my use of the conceit of gods to characterize the young men I'd sought to immortalize. Of course, Tod had the hots for Mel, too, and was, therefore, not an entirely impartial critic. Indeed, he was in the midst of writing his own portrait of Mel, no doubt designed to correct my version and – who knows? – perhaps win our hero's heart.

"If any of my boyfriends read it, they'll kill me," Mel said dejectedly. I imagined a litter of Mel's past, present, and future boyfriends scattered around town in various apartment towers turning the pages at this very moment. "What if Jason sees it?" Mel asked.

I'd forgotten about Jason. He was Mel's great ex-, and my portrait of him was decidedly unflattering as I not only recounted the tales of their lovemaking that Mel had passed on, but had worked myself up into a lather imagining the details of how Mel had penetrated the young man's macho facade, tying Jason's hands behind his back with a leather thong, and forcing whimpering cries of pleasure from his throat as he plugged him with savage affection.

But then I remembered, with a grateful sigh, that Jason was in Los Angeles, New Orleans, wherever. Mel was not about to be placated by mere geography.

"You wanted me to write about you," I reminded him.

"Yeah, but not like this," Mel said.

For an instant, all sentimentalities aside, I glimpsed the gap between our lives. Anyone who whispers his amorous adventures to a storyteller is doomed to hear them repeated as betrayed confidences. Mel couldn't possibly have known that; I did, but was in the grip of a greater power than desire.

We were at the beginning of months of icy estrangement. Naturally, all of our friends would gleefully get into the act. A stream of emissaries eventually made their way to the Rut, allegedly on my behalf, but since, like Tod, they too had the hots for Mel, such missions could only be subverted by the diplomats' own desiring agendas.

Now, the critic-characters began appearing with increasing frequency. On the phone, in the mail, at my elbow when I looked up from the melting icecubes in my drink. People who had merited but a line in the text, others who only imagined themselves to be in it, walk-ons, extras, everyone had a literary opinion.

I began to feel like Grace Metalious after she wrote *Peyton Place*. She was an author from my childhood who had burst asunder the prudish 1950s with a potboiler-*à-clef* about a small town in New England apparently seething with lust. The real townspeople hated her afterwards. Metalious had taken to drink. She came to a bad end, I seem to recall.

I WAKE DISTRESSED around 4:30 a.m. Wrap myself in soft fabrics – old flannelette, worn denim, moccasins. I think about the particular people who had moved me, whose lives ought to be written, whose stories deserved telling.

But why? There were, of course, superficial and sufficient reasons. But finally the reason is – and though it rings like a cliche, I'm nonetheless enamoured of its sound – *or else they will be lost.*

Did I imagine myself rescuing souls condemned to limbo? The wondrous Catholics, seeking remission for their dead, try to shorten the stays of the departed who have been consigned to purgatory, as if they are their elderly relatives who have won a holiday in Mexico or Hawaii on a game show or in the lottery, but are trapped in faceless airports from which they can be released only through the intercessionary prayers of their kin and friends.

As I ponder, I can hear the chirping of the first dawn birds in the laurel hedge outside. Whatever might be left of the full moon is either gone or misted over. It is an hour of death, well before morning.

Consider even someone as fleeting as this person – found in a passage in Proust (though I take the liberty of retransposing the genders) – encountered on the little train from Balbec to one of those interminable social occasions at la Raspelière for which the young Marcel lived in those days: an arresting youth from whose "magnolia skin," dark eyes, lithe shape, he could not take his eyes.

The boy opens a window, smokes a cigarette. "I would have liked to say to him: 'Come with us to the Verdurins' or 'Give me your name and address.' I answered: 'No, fresh air doesn't bother me'." And the next day, Marcel exclaims to his beloved Albert, of that beautiful boy: "I should so like to see him again." "'Don't worry, one always sees people again,' replied Albert. In this particular instance, he was wrong; I never saw him again, and never identified the handsome boy with the cigarette. . .But I never forgot him. I find myself at times, when I think of him, seized by a wild longing. But these recurrences of desire oblige us to reflect that if we wish to rediscover these boys with the same pleasure we must also return to the year which has since been followed by ten others in the course of which his bloom has faded. We sometimes find a person again, but we cannot abolish time." Whoever he was – and the point perhaps is simply that *he was* – he would be lost to us but for the accident of Proust writing about his ineffable beauty.

THE KINETIC MAGIC that dictated the return of *Buddy's* characters had become such a mundane occurrence that I was barely surprised when I picked up the phone one weekend morning about a week after I'd seen Mel and heard again the sexual velvet in Bret's voice. For several years, I hadn't seen or heard from the youth who had played Eros in my tapestry.

Naturally, he can't see me; he's only in town for the weekend, there's a plane to catch; yes, he still lives in Edmonton, married, a two-year-old daughter, job; but there was some sort of auto accident about a year before; and this brief trip is in some unexplained way connected with sorting out the effects of it. He has to get a pencil and paper to write down the name of my book; in the background, I hear the usual electronic blur of music, TV, a name being uttered. He must be in the suburban apartment tower of the man he once lived with.

Afterwards, I re-read the "Eros" section of *Buddy's* in which Bret appears. Glance at the address I've written down. He's just moved (of course), no phone yet. I try to remember who told me a couple of weeks ago that it would be impossible to really feel romantic love again. It was Tod. He was telling me the story of a younger man, in his late twenties, who had fallen in love with him. Tod rolled his eyes, flicked his snub nose, giggled mischievously, as if to say: not *that* abyss again. Outside, it's spring. The sun is burning away the morning haze. By noon, it'll be hot; people will fill the beaches.

Bret called back at six. The plane wasn't leaving until morning. I drove out to the burbs. We went to a cocktail lounge in the new monster shopping mall called Metrotown (it had already been dubbed Heterotown in the gay bars). The lounge was one of those places where a two-piece band plays country and western, people dance, and a casino goes on in the next red-and-gold-flocked-wallpaper room.

He was wearing a white tank-top T-shirt and tight, pale jeans. He sported a big corolla of curly blond hair, a lean muscularity (from working in a warehouse), and was sunburnt after a day spent at the nude beach with the man he used to live with and the man's current live-in. The total effect Bret gives off is somewhat desperate.

The story he's brought me here to listen to is about "the

accident." There's a long lead-up about his relationship with Alison, the women with whom he left Vancouver – how many years ago was it? That long? Anyway, there are sporadic habitations, predictable breakups, some episodes of battering and fist-through-the-wall stuff which make me cringe, and finally, the daughter.

The punchline is that the accident was no accident. He was riding to work on a bike. He saw the car from more than a block away. He sped up. The details blur. He had or hadn't gone through the windshield. In any case, the suicide didn't work. There was, instead, plenty of blood, coma, some temporary brain scrambling to add to his emotional desperation. And after the partial physical recovery, a further breakdown, psych ward at the university hospital, rehab, etc. The C&W tunes oozed through Bret's tale.

The reason I'm here is because he's written a lot of this down – big loose-leaf diaries and pages of poems which he now hauls out of a leather shoulder bag, and which I'm supposed to read, right now. I can see that he's rather painfully nuts, still hyper, and the intensity, as before, seems to me narcissistic – even when apparently displaced, as onto his baby daughter. His small blue eyes, with pinhole black pupils, look dead.

Later, parked in the circular driveway at the foot of the tower where I'm dropping him off, there's an odd moment. The writing, which I read while sipping a flat beer, was too vague, abstract, and asexual to suit my tastes, though I thought that my friend George might find some of the poems interesting.

Bret's telling me about being at the nude beach that afternoon, and I'm picking up the sense that he got horny. I mean, why go to the nude beach without feeling some kind of desire? Yet, in one of those classic mixed messages he's insisting that, with respect to his bisexuality, he now keeps the homo part locked safely inside. Which means that he still goes to gay bars in Edmonton, and drives men crazy.

Because of his facial bone structure and the tautness of his body, Bret's still temptingly attractive, even though time and pain have worn away some of the beauty. In fact, what I'm picking up is not only that he got horny at the beach, but that he's horny right now, talking to me, or remembering the afternoon. He's glancing surreptitiously at his watch, calculating whether it's too late (since there's a plane to catch in the morning). I could tip it, with a word, a hint. And it's true, I'd like to hear his confessions and cries of desire just once more. But he's too scary to desire. I'd have to be careful not only of his sunburnt skin, but of his fragile psyche. Finally, I couldn't be sure that it was him who had decided, and not something else. I let it pass.

Afterwards, there was a brief, inconclusive correspondence. He read *Buddy's* – painfully, because of the mental scrambling from the accident – but denied that it had anything to do with him, with his body. Reading Bret's language, I remember the reasons why I'm not living with him.

IT WAS ONLY after Sidney's death (more than a year after the time of the events I'm writing about here) that it occurred to me that he was the sole person to appear in *Buddy's* who was genuinely gratified to be there. My friend George, the undeniable star of the book, grudgingly and graciously put up with having been characterized, perhaps mildly flattered by the attention it brought him, but also annoyed that people hadn't figured out that it would be easier to simply read his poems. Sidney, however, who had sought respect much of his life, felt himself to be justly regarded in those pages.

There had been one significant afternoon between us, years before, in the Ambassador pub. I remember the sunlight that flashed in from the summer street each time someone came through the foyer doors into the bar. We were, of course, casually cruising the room as we talked. Perhaps it was that that led Sidney to lament the dilemma of how to value the young men there whose value was set by hustling.

"But it's simple," I said offhandedly. "They're humans, boys, persons, that's all you have to remember."

Sidney seemed taken by that small bit of inadvertent wisdom. Indeed, the idea may have originated with George, now that I think of it.

"Of course," I added, "a world that makes them stand on streetcorners isn't fair."

"In a fair world," Sidney replied, "they'd see our beauty for itself."

To someone passing down the aisle between the terrycloth covered tables where we sat having a beer, Sidney and I must have looked like two rather fat, middle-aged men waiting for evening. For some reason, that conversation stayed with Sidney, as if it had solved a problem for him. And in his references to it, it stayed with me, also.

Now, on the eighth floor AIDS wing of St. Paul's Hospital, Sidney is wearing a transparent plastic mask hooked to an oxygen machine. From the window of the room, there's a panorama of downtown Vancouver, the pale green roof of the Hotel Vancouver a familiar landmark, the gold-flecked pink glass of a nearby office tower shimmering in the sun. When Sidney stands up by the bedside, still hooked to the oxygen, he turns from me and unceremoniously drops his hospital pajama bottoms to pee in a plastic pitcher – and I can't help but notice that the cheeks of his ass are greatly shrunken, the flesh hanging in elephantine folds. Even as we maintain an unruffled patter, I feel the wham of mortality against my chest.

IT WAS THE NIGHT of the September full moon, about six months after *Buddy's* had come out. As I dashed through the stalled traffic, ambling toward the Rut, the great orb in the sky was hazily pillowed in clouds. I'd finished my book about local politics and the college season had begun again (the parents hadn't, after all, picketed).

Inside, Mel was behind the bar, wearing spandex mid-thigh-length shorts that spectacularly featured his basket. And though he was simultaneously mixing drinks, talking on the phone, and bantering with some customers, did I pick up an instant micro-signal sent my way whose emotional waves weren't consonant with the months of frigidity between us?

Greg's friend Mark – in powder blue tight jeans (no loose pleated trousers or baggy shorts for him), with a mashed boxer's nose and thick lips (the kind models go to plastic surgeons to get) – was standing at the pool table, waiting for his opponent to come out of the john before making his shot.

There were pretty young men everywhere, including a charmingly fem kid who seemed to be a one-person Porn Corner, wearing jeans he'd been positively poured into as he passionately and unfurtively groped the nearest nearby youth. Yes, there they were, scattered about the room, all of them lip-synching to a disco tune on the sound system called, "Boys, Boys, Boys."

In the intervening months, the stream of characters-cum-literary critics had tailed off. So, that was over, more or less. About the only one I'd been spared – in fact, the only one who I felt guilty about – was Mel's old flame, Jason. But Jason, thank god, had safely disappeared into the maw of L.A., New Orleans, wherever.

Naturally, that was the moment he chose to appear in the recessed doorway of the john. Jason picked up the cue that was standing alongside the chalkboard, and was about to take up his match with Mark when he spotted me. He made a bee-line in my direction, a familiar long-time-no-see grin creasing his face, hand extended, then firmly pumping mine as he heartily congratulated me on *Buddy's*. When the impatient players called him back to the table, I went to the bar for a drink.

Mel had already poured me a freebie, resuming an old gift-custom of earlier days. Jason had apparently read it and, Mel reported, "he doesn't hate me." Indeed, more than that, for when I made my way back through the room to Jason, he proposed that the three of us – himself, Mel, and I – sign a copy of *Buddy's* so that he could send it to his and Mel's mutual older friend in L.A., Gene. "He took my confession," Jason explains, putting it in the terms acquired by a boy with a good Catholic upbringing, "while you were taking Mel's." When I suggest that he could go around the corner to the late-night bookstore on movie row and pick up a copy for us to sign, he's gone in a flash.

But the point – the blessed point – comes later, as we're standing by the wall, along the little chest-high shelf on which we set our drinks. We're idly admiring Mark as we make chit-chat. Jason's now working as a stockbroker on the local exchange. You couldn't tell it at this hour, glancing at his tousled hair, black T-shirt, intimate studly style.

Then, apropos of nothing in particular, and beginning haltingly, Jason says that there's a "criticism" he must make of the book. He sounds almost apologetic.

"Do you remember the part where you say Mel tied my hands behind my back and I was on my belly and came rubbing against the sheets while he fucked me?" Jason asks.

Do I remember? How could I forget? "Of course," I say.

"It wasn't a leather thong that he tied my hands with."

"It wasn't?" I repeat, dumbfoundedly.

"It was electrical cord."

"Electrical cord?" I echo.

"You know, the rubber cord from an electric razor."

"Yeah, yeah," I absently mutter. It's beginning to dawn on me. Then, even more precisely:

"And I was on my *back*," Jason says.

Are you with me? *I.e.*, Jason is simply telling me what happened. Good god, not a criticism, but a correction, a crucial correction to ensure the truth and accuracy of this testament of love.

"Were your hands tied behind your back or over your head?" I ask.

There is absolutely nothing between us, nothing held back – this young man of 25 or so and I have the transparent intimacy of both having loved Mel, of both having submitted ourselves – many times.

"Over my head," Jason reports. The cord was tied to the

metal bedstead in the Guildford Hotel on Robson Street (I had been there once myself), and held Jason's hands in place over his head while he lay on his back, his legs in the air, over Mel's shoulders, as he squirmingly imagined his embarrassment should a mutual friend come through the door to discover that his butch cover story concealed a boy begging to be fucked. Jason blew his wad without his dick being so much as touched. His cum gushed onto his rippled belly solely from the force of Mel's cock buried in his ass. I marvel at this rarest of gifts, the literal truth.

AT THE END of the epilogue, the author at last understands that conventional phrase which concludes so many prefaces, whereby all others are absolved, and it is declared that "whatever faults remain are my own."

About the author
STAN PERSKY teaches philosophy and political studies at Capilano
College in North Vancouver, British Columbia.

About the bar
BUDDY'S, at 1018 Burnaby Street in Vancouver, B.C., opened in
spring 1982 and closed in summer 1988.

Printed in Canada